# FIELDS TO FORTUNE

Fields to Fortune

*The True Story of How a Farmhand Built a Global Empire*

Moses Heredia

©2025 All Rights Reserved. No portion of this book may be reproduced, stored in a retrieval system, or transmitted in any form or by any means—electronic, mechanical, photocopy, recording, scanning, or other—except for brief quotations in critical reviews or articles without the prior permission of the author.

Published by Game Changer Publishing

Paperback ISBN: 978-1-966659-94-5

Hardcover ISBN: 978-1-966659-95-2

Digital ISBN: 978-1-966659-96-9

www.GameChangerPublishing.com

# DEDICATION

*This book is dedicated to my mom. Because of you, I'm in business. You taught me to never fear, the importance of keeping to myself, and the value of being careful with whom I trust. Your guidance to bless others, as you are blessed, fueled my passion for charity.*

*You instilled in me a deep belief in God and in myself. Because of you, I'm a successful businessman, a better man, and one with a big heart.*

# READ THIS FIRST

Just to say thanks for buying and reading my book, I would like to give you a free gift, no strings attached!

**Scan the QR Code Here:**

# FIELDS TO FORTUNE
THE TRUE STORY OF HOW A FARMHAND
BUILT A GLOBAL EMPIRE

MOSES HEREDIA

# FOREWORD

There has been much said the last few years about exceptionalism. Unfortunately, I have not seen a good definition or description of exceptionalism. To that end, I will take the risk and throw out some thoughts.

First, I believe an exceptional person is one who sees an opportunity and takes it. They are generally fully aware of the risks of failure, but the chance at success is too great to pass up.

Second, I believe an exceptional person has an exceptional sense of morality and truth. They will not compromise on what they believe or how they pursue their convictions.

Third, they have an unshakable commitment to honor and loyalty. When they have committed to another person, they will not budge or compromise.

Fourth, they have a very high standard of achievement, and they know how to pass that standard on to others with whom they associate; they will not settle for second best.

Sadly, in seventy-eight years of living, I have rarely known such a person. Fortunately, in 2004, I met Moses Heredia and worked with him for the next eighteen years.

It was he who showed me what exceptionalism is all about.

– Donald B. Kennedy
MBA Management Services

# CONTENTS

Introduction     xiii

### PART ONE
## THE GRIND

1. From Humble Beginnings     3
2. A New Start in the States     9
3. Learning By Example     17
4. Doing Right, Every Day     23
5. Work Was First     29
6. Discipline Shaped Me     35
    The Grind Got Me Here     45

### PART TWO
## GOD IS REAL

7. The Wakeup Call     51
8. A One-Way Ticket to California     55
9. To the Bank, Not the Bars     61
10. Determination Before Defeat     67
11. Hard Work Pays Off     71
12. Paying It Forward     81
    God is Real     91

### PART THREE
## GET A GOAL AND GO ALL IN

13. Following My Gut     97
14. Growing From the Ground Up     101
15. Betrayal Is Inevitable     107
16. Overcoming Obstacles     111
    Get a Goal and Go All In     117

### PART FOUR
## GO GLOBAL

17. Facing Grief     121
18. Give Back     127
19. A Vision for the Future     133

    Moses's Proverbs To Live By     139
    Perspective From Friends     143
    Thank You For Reading My Book!     149

# INTRODUCTION

This is a story about God, faith, and going all in. I moved to California with nothing but a dream and a couple of dollars in my pocket, trusting that the journey would lead me to where I am today.

I hope my story becomes a blueprint for the impact you can make. It's not about where you start—it's about the faith you have in God and your willingness to stay dedicated to the grind, no matter how hard it gets.

How many of you want to leave a legacy, serve the less fortunate, and create opportunities for others? Here's the hard truth: life has told you that you can't.

Fear has told you not to take risks. Maybe you've told yourself, I'm just an immigrant. I don't have the education. You might feel like success is out of reach because you weren't born into wealth, or you don't feel you have the right skin color or background to make it.

But I'm here to tell you—*yes, you can.*

I'm here to show you how I went from working the fields of

## INTRODUCTION

Hobbs, New Mexico, to becoming the CEO of Global Processing Systems.

You can bet on yourself. You can create the life you've dreamed of. You can make the money, you can make the impact, and yes, you can leave a legacy.

I'm going to teach you four life-changing concepts that I call my **4G's: God, Goals, Grind,** and **Global.**

I'm here to tell you that The Grind got me here—that God is Real—if you Set a Goal—and Go All In, you too can Go Global.

# PART ONE
# THE GRIND

# CHAPTER 1
# FROM HUMBLE BEGINNINGS

*"And let us not grow weary of doing good, for in due season we shall reap if we do not give up."*
— Galatians 6:9 NIV

My mom passed away in 2004, but she's still one of the most influential people in my life. Born in the 1940s, she was a proud, private woman, so it wasn't until after she passed that I fully understood the depth of her story.

She was born in a small village on the rural outskirts of Ojinaga, Chihuahua, to a large farming family with fourteen siblings. She grew up in a world where survival depended on the land, her life one of hard labor: farming cantaloupe, vegetables, wheat, and beans—even raising bees for honey. My grandfather, whom I never had the chance to meet, worked tirelessly to keep food on the table, while my mother and her siblings had to forgo school to help, walking door-to-door to sell what produce they could.

What they didn't sell would be preserved for later seasons, or repurposed. The beeswax from their hives was recycled into candles as their only source of light, and water from the river was boiled to make it drinkable. As you can imagine, their house was small, and at night, five or six of the girls would sleep in a single bed, while my grandparents slept on the floor.

Despite this poverty, my mom and her family were rich in the strength of their community. Living so far out in the country, they had no choice but to rely on each other. Surrounding farmers would share remedies, lend a hand, and help each other survive.

Without a formal education, my mom learned everything she knew from those around her. From her mother, she learned to cook, feeding a large family. From her father, she learned the art of entrepreneurship, the value of hard work, and how to market and sell their crops. It was because of these skills that, after his death, when she was just twenty years old, she decided to venture out on her own to fulfill her dream of opening a restaurant, which we'll talk about in a later chapter, determined to build a better life for her family.

Her ambition and drive were unmistakable. She was driven, motivated, and determined. I believe without those three qualities, you're just chasing the wind and taking up space. My mom was always driven. She was constantly thinking of ways to hustle and make a living. No matter what obstacles she faced, she always found a way to keep moving forward. She was motivated by the desire to provide a better life for her children, and knowing the hardships she endured only deepened my appreciation for how hard she worked to give us a different kind of future.

Despite the challenges, she never saw her circumstances as a source of shame. Instead, she used her upbringing as fuel to build a better life. That deep desire for something more, something better, became a part of who she was—and it was passed down to me. It was in her DNA, and it became a part of mine.

While I didn't have the hardships she did, my childhood wasn't without its challenges. Like her, I was raised with a strong sense of structure. "Have something to do, or find something to do," she'd say. There was always work to be done, always something to learn. She instilled in me the same qualities that helped her overcome obstacles.

But what stands out most about her was her determination. She didn't care if she lacked the skills or didn't speak the language—she would dive in and figure it out. She was a risk-taker, unafraid to seize an opportunity, even if she didn't know exactly how she would make it work. If a door was open, she walked through it. If it wasn't, she found a way around it. That determination is where I got mine from.

I also learned something else from her: discipline. It's not just about working hard or being driven; it's about doing the work consistently. Whether it's hitting the gym, sticking to a diet, working long hours, or simply showing up every day, it all takes discipline. That's how my mom lived. She was disciplined in everything she did: the way she worked, the way she cared for us, and the way she hustled to provide. And it goes to show that if you can stay disciplined and maintain a routine, success is inevitable.

Galatians 6:9 says, "And let us not grow weary of doing good, for in due season we shall reap if we do not give up." This verse speaks to everything my mom taught me. These days, everything is about speed—quick fixes, fast results—but success doesn't come that way. It's like growing a garden. You plant the seed, and you nurture it, you water it, you tend to it, and you don't expect it to bear fruit overnight. Building something meaningful takes time. It takes consistency. It takes not growing weary when the results don't come immediately. Success is earned day by day, week by week, year by year.

In business, as in life, there are no shortcuts. I've been at this for over twenty-one years, and nothing came fast. It was a constant process of scaling, little by little. But the key is never giving up. Even when it feels like progress is slow or that you're not seeing the fruits of your labor yet, you keep going, because in due season, you will reap what you've sown.

The apostle Paul was speaking to the church in Galatia, a community that was beginning to grow weary because their goals of reaching people for Christ hadn't yet materialized. Paul encouraged them, as he does all of us: Don't give up. Be patient, keep pushing forward, because the harvest will come. And the only way you'll reach that harvest is if you stay driven, motivated, and determined.

My mom exemplified this every single day of her life. Despite everything she faced, she didn't grow weary. She was motivated by her dream of a better life for her family, and she was determined to make it happen, no matter how long it took. And like Paul urged the church in Galatia, she never gave up. She watered her garden, nurtured it, and continued to move forward. And eventually, she reaped the rewards. I believe the same is true for all of us. Whatever your dream is, whatever your goal, do not grow weary of doing good. Keep nurturing it, keep working at it, and stay consistent. The harvest will come. The journey isn't always easy, but it's always worth it if you keep going.

What I want you to take away from this chapter is to imagine, for a moment, that you're living in a situation where you have nothing. No money in the bank. No food on the table. No new shoes on your feet. Now, maybe you've never been in this position, and I hope you never have to be, but think about what it would feel like. The desperation. The struggle. That's the reality many people face, and it's the kind of mentality that comes with living in survival mode.

Now picture yourself in the jungle. But instead of being the prey, you're the lion. You're hungry. You're desperate. And if you don't hunt, you don't survive.

The lion doesn't stop hunting. No matter how hard it gets, no matter how long it takes, the lion keeps going because survival is at stake. That's the mentality you need when you're working from a place of nothing. When you're struggling, when you're fighting just to survive, you have to push harder, think smarter, and keep moving forward.

That was the mentality my mom grew up with. She was born into poverty, and every single day, she had to hunt for survival. She wasn't waiting for opportunities to come to her; she created her own. She was always in search of the next meal, the next dollar, the next opportunity. Life forced her to think like that—survive or perish. She didn't just survive, though. She thrived.

If you're struggling, if you feel like you don't have enough, I want you to remember that you're a lion. Your hunger, your drive, your determination to get ahead—that's the grind that will carry you through. So dig deep. Tap into that mentality. And remember that if my mom kept going, kept searching, kept fighting, you can do the same.

You have the same drive within you. All you need to do is tap into it. Like a lion, keep hunting. Because in the end, it's the strong, the determined, the relentless who survive and thrive.

> **Axiom:** BE DRIVEN, BE MOTIVATED, AND BE DETERMINED.
>
> **Bible Verse:** *"And let us not grow weary of doing good, for in due season we shall reap if we do not give up."*
> — Galatians 6:9 NIV

# CHAPTER 2
# A NEW START IN THE STATES

*"For I know the plans I have for you, declares the Lord, plans to prosper you and not to harm you, plans to give you hope and a future."*
— Jeremiah 29:11 NIV

My mom was one of the oldest in her family, and after her father passed away, she felt a deep sense of responsibility to help. At just twenty years old, living on the outskirts of the city near the farm where she grew up, right on the border of Texas and Mexico, she found and rented a place that was part restaurant, part bar, with small hotels and cabins scattered around the grounds. She took on the daunting task of running the restaurant and, in addition, began renting out the surrounding cabins.

It quickly became clear that this was far too much for her to handle alone. So, she enlisted her siblings to work in roles that best suited their skills—waitstaff, cooks—while she took charge of the business side, managing operations and developing recipes that reflected her passion for cooking. She used the profits from the restaurant to send food and groceries back home to support her entire family. It was a massive responsibility, but it was a smart move. At the time, many Americans traveling to Mexico would stop at her restaurant for food, drinks, and a place to stay. That included my father.

My father, an American citizen, was just seventeen years old when they met. He came into the restaurant regularly because his own family farm was not far from my mother's. Soon, he got to know the people around town, including my mom, and learned who she was. According to my father, it was love at first sight, though my mom wasn't as quick to feel the same way. She was focused on her work and had no interest in starting a relationship. But every time he came to town, he would stop by the restaurant, order something, and linger until she finished her workday. To avoid him, she even started using the back door, but he was persistent—if not that day, then the next, and the next.

Finally, after weeks of this, my mom, clearly frustrated, told him that he was too young for her and that she didn't think he was ready to commit in the ways she needed. But my father didn't back down. He told her he didn't care about the age difference—he admired her intelligence and the way she carried herself. Slowly, she gave in, and they began dating. And not long after, they fell in love.

I love this story because my father's persistence and intention embody the belief that everything happens for a reason. Nothing is a coincidence, but rather, the result of determination—a quality that both my parents shared, and one that they passed on to me.

My parents spent many long nights talking about their future together, including the future of the restaurant. While the business was bringing in enough to support their family, my mom had hit a ceiling in terms of income and began searching for other opportunities. My father, still traveling between West Texas and Mexico, showed her that just across the border, the value of the dollar was much higher, and there was more opportunity to be had.

It took some convincing to get my mom to step away from the security of the restaurant she had worked so hard to build. But, once again, she took a leap of faith and decided to move to the United States—but there was a catch. She didn't have American citizenship or proper documentation. My father, however, promised that he would take care of it. He told her to trust him, because they were in it together.

At this point, it's important to mention that my father was also taking a huge risk. Coming from a similar background—one of six children—he hadn't received a formal education either, and spent his youth working on the family farm, much like my mother had. Back then, education was a luxury, and his family didn't have the resources to give him that. This shared experience is a part of what drew them to each other. They both believed in each other, and that mutual belief was the foundation for their success.

So, my mother trusted my father, and together, they made the move to Hobbs, New Mexico, where I would later be born and raised. My father went ahead to find a job, and my mom followed. It was a new journey for both of them, but especially for my mom, who didn't speak English and had no formal education.

At first, the language barrier limited the jobs she could take, but my mother was resourceful. She taught herself English on the side and soon took on a role as an independent contractor, connecting farmers with field laborers. For several months out of the year, she worked alongside the laborers, harvesting whatever was in season —vegetables, nuts, cotton. Eventually, when she was ready, she opened her own restaurant again, followed by a second-hand store.

There was nothing that could stop her. Even though she didn't speak English and didn't have the education many people thought she needed to succeed, my mom just made things happen. This is where my admiration for her really grew. She didn't let the roadblocks that society set up for her—being a woman, being an immigrant, not knowing the language—stand in her way. She saw no obstacles, only opportunities. And over time, she became the breadwinner in our family, earning more than my father. She even sent money back to her mother and siblings in Mexico. She ran the household, called the shots, and continued to do so even after having my siblings and me. She managed to juggle multiple jobs, all while making sure we were well-educated, well-fed, and well-dressed. Everything she went without, she made sure we had.

I remember people knocking on the door, saying, "I don't have enough money to pay my electricity bill. Can I borrow some money?" My mom would not only give them the money but also groceries she had in her cupboard. She would go above and beyond, and I admire her for that. I am now able to do the same.

From the very beginning, my mother was a goal-setter and a trendsetter. She would dive into every opportunity headfirst, whether it was starting a business, moving to a new country, or learning English. If she set her mind to something, she made it happen. There was no "maybe," no "I can't." It was always, "I will. And that mindset—the ability to set goals and believe that you can achieve them—was the most important lesson I learned from her.

It's not enough to just want something. You have to work for it, plan for it, and believe that you deserve it. And this is where many people fall short. They may have dreams, but they don't believe in themselves enough to chase them. It's easy to say, "I want to be successful," but much harder to do the work and believe in your ability to make it happen.

Even before I understood the concept of admiration, I looked up to my mother. Her ambition, her persistence, her refusal to let anything hold her back—these are the qualities I admired. She was a doer, not a dreamer. And like mother, like son, I've had to do the same in building my own business. I can look back now and realize that the lessons she taught me—about hard work, commitment, and believing in yourself—are the foundation of everything I've accomplished.

Here's the thing: in the face of adversity, my mother identified her purpose and believed in herself—and those two things are the most important first steps toward success. To feel fulfilled, you must first identify your purpose. We are all born with a unique mark we can leave on the world. And not only do we have to believe we have a purpose, we have to believe that we are capable of carrying it out. If we don't believe we can achieve it, we won't. It's as simple as that.

After so many years, in my forties, I thought, *What is my purpose in life?*

I went to dinner with my pastor, and I was like, "Listen. I have no idea what my gift is or what I'm doing here, but I know I have a purpose, and I need to find that purpose."

One of the things he said was, "Moses, you're doing your purpose. You're living your gift." He continued, "You give back to so many people, and you do so much. You're helping everyone employed by you, so you're *doing* your purpose. Continue doing what you're doing."

At the time, I didn't understand. I was just doing what I was taught—to help people. It wasn't until years later that I understood. I talk to people every day about becoming better. I talk to people about God, about goals, about the grind, and about making a global impact. That is my gift. My gift is to help people, to inspire people, to give people a better lifestyle, and I've done that with my company.

This reminds me of Jeremiah 29:11—*"For I know the plans I have for you, declares the Lord, plans to prosper you and not to harm you, plans to give you hope and a future."*

This verse is powerful because it speaks to the fact that there is a plan for each of us, a unique purpose laid out before us. But it's not just about knowing that plan exists—it's about choosing to believe that you can walk in it. God has given each of us a purpose, but we must actively choose to pursue it. It's a partnership between our belief and action, where we walk through the doors He opens for us. The opportunities are there, but we have to choose to step through them, just like my mother did time and time again.

Now, for those of you who are reading this and don't believe in yourselves, let me speak to you directly: I get it. It's hard to see the way forward when you don't feel confident or ready. But you have to believe in yourself before anyone else will. If you don't have that foundational self-belief, it doesn't matter how many books you read or courses you take. Without believing in your own abilities, the work won't be worth the risk. If you don't believe in yourself, no one else will either.

In the early days of my career, I remember walking away from my corporate job without a single doubt that I was going to succeed. I was all in and of the belief that I would get there, no matter what.

It's not enough to just "want" success—you have to work at it. You have to set goals, you have to show up every day, and you have to be consistent. Many people fail in business because they aren't willing to put in the hours. They see the flash and pizzazz of success on social media and think it happens overnight, but it doesn't.

This is where discipline comes in. If you don't have the ability to push through when times get tough, you'll get discouraged. And that's why many entrepreneurs fail in the first few years. They don't understand that success takes time; they don't understand that it's a marathon, not a sprint.

I often remind my team to Be Positive, Productive, and Proactive. Do these three things every single day, and you'll find your purpose—or perhaps, you'll realize that you've already found it. It's all about taking productive, proactive steps toward your goals and staying positive along the way.

Take it from me: it doesn't matter where you come from. It doesn't matter your background, your challenges, or your struggles. We are all born equal. It's what you do with the opportunities that matter. My mother started with nothing, and look at what she built. I started with nothing, and here I am. I didn't have an education. I wasn't born with a silver spoon in my mouth, and neither were my grandparents or my ancestors. Just because your parents are not wealthy doesn't mean you can't change things. Success is about belief. Your goals don't discriminate—they're just waiting for you to claim them.

If you've made it this far and still feel unsure, know this: It's never too late to start believing in yourself. It's about making a decision—to trust yourself, to believe in your ability to succeed, and to keep pushing forward. The road is yours to take.

So look in the mirror today and ask yourself: Do I believe in myself? If you don't, start by setting small goals and working towards them. Keep pushing, keep believing, and you'll start seeing the results. Success is waiting for you, but you have to believe it's possible first.

---

**Axiom:** BELIEVE IN YOURSELF.

**Bible Verse:** *"For I know the plans I have for you, declares the Lord, plans to prosper you and not to harm you, plans to give you hope and a future."*
— Jeremiah 29:11 NIV

# CHAPTER 3
# LEARNING BY EXAMPLE

*"Therefore, as God's chosen people, holy and dearly loved, clothe yourself with compassion, kindness, humility, gentleness, and patience."*
— Colossians 3:12 NIV

My mother was, without a doubt, one of the most compassionate people I've ever known. She was tough, no question, but her heart was even bigger than her determination. Her compassion wasn't just about feeling for people; it was about doing something to help them. Whether it was family, friends, neighbors, or strangers, my mother's ability to step in and help others was unmatched. And what's amazing is that this compassion wasn't just a one-time act—it was a consistent part of who she was, day in and day out.

She wasn't just compassionate toward her own family, either. Of course, she always made sure her family was cared for, but her kindness extended far beyond that. Growing up, I remember people coming to our house, asking for help with one thing or another—whether it was a place to stay, financial assistance, or simply someone to listen. And my mother would always lend a hand, no questions asked.

One of the most impactful ways my mother showed compassion was through her work. She didn't just employ people; she gave them opportunities. My mother hired many undocumented workers, many of whom came from families that struggled to survive. She helped them get work, but she also helped them gain legal status. I remember my sister, Cenia, and me helping her type up letters to get them notarized to submit to the government. By proving that these workers were employed and contributing to society, she helped them gain legal residency.

Of course, it didn't stop with work. My mother would regularly travel back to Mexico, taking clothes, food, and necessities to relatives and neighbors who were struggling. I have memories of her packing up boxes of things and driving five hours to Chihuahua to drop them off to strangers. She would donate to schools, churches, and local organizations, always looking for ways to help the less fortunate.

But what stands out most to me is that she didn't do these things for recognition. She wasn't doing it to boast about how many people she'd helped. She did it because she genuinely cared. She understood what it meant to struggle, what it meant to build a life from nothing. To her, compassion wasn't about what other people saw; it was about doing the right thing when no one was watching. And that, to me, is integral to true success.

Beverly Hills Dinner, September 2024: President Donald J. Trump and Moses Heredia

I once saw a video of President Donald J. Trump at church. He didn't know he was being filmed, but in the video, he reaches into his pocket, pulls out a few bills, and quietly slips them into the offering basket. It wasn't a large amount, but what struck me was how discreetly he did it. There was no fanfare, no desire for recognition—just a simple, private act of generosity. That's what success with compassion looks like. It wasn't about making sure the world knew about his good deed, but instead about quietly making a difference.

As I mentioned, my mother's compassion was the same. She didn't do things for social media likes or public praise. Her actions just reflected who she was—a person who wanted to help others succeed, just as she had fought to succeed herself. Her story shows us that success is not just about reaching the top and staying there. It's about lifting others as you climb.

You don't have to be a billionaire to lead with compassion. You don't have to have fame or fortune to make an impact. Compassion is something that anyone, at any level, can practice. Whether you're an entrepreneur, a business leader, or someone trying to make a difference in your community, compassion cultivates connection. It creates trust. It builds loyalty. It's the foundation for lasting relationships, whether with employees, customers, or strangers.

The Bible speaks about this kind of compassion, too. In Colossians 3, Paul tells believers, *"Therefore, as God's chosen people, holy and dearly loved, clothe yourselves with compassion, kindness, humility, gentleness, and patience."* Why does Paul emphasize compassion so much? Because God was so compassionate, Jesus himself was compassionate with everyone. Without compassion, you can't be humble or patient. It's the key that unlocks all the rest and the foundation of community.

And let's not forget the story of the Good Samaritan, which Jesus used to illustrate the power of compassion in action. A man was beaten by thieves and left on the side of the road, and while others passed him by, only one man stopped to help. He bandaged his wounds, took him to an inn, and made sure he had the care he needed. Jesus used this parable to teach that true compassion isn't just about feeling pity. It's about taking action, even when it's inconvenient or doesn't bring you any personal gain. The Samaritan's compassion led to real change for the injured man, and it's a perfect example of how compassion leads to real success.

My mother's story shows us that success, in its truest sense, is not just about what we can achieve for ourselves—it's about what we can do for others. Compassion helps us lift others up and asks for nothing in return. When you lead with compassion, you create a ripple effect that can change lives. It's this kind of leadership, this kind of success, that makes an impact.

In business and in life, compassion creates an environment where people feel valued. When you lead with compassion, people want to work with you. They want to help you build something.

Whether it's giving someone a job, helping a client solve a problem, or being there for your team when they need support, compassion builds trust. And trust is the foundation of any successful relationship, personal or professional.

So, just as my mother's compassion shaped the lives of those around her, so too can compassion shape your own path to success. You don't need to be wealthy to practice compassion. You just need to care about others, and act on that care. When you lead with compassion, you don't just build success for yourself—you help others build their success, too. And that's a legacy worth striving for.

---

**Axiom:** BE COMPASSIONATE.

**Bible Verse:** *"Therefore, as God's chosen people, holy and dearly loved, clothe yourself with compassion, kindness, humility, gentleness, and patience."* — Colossians 3:12 NIV

# CHAPTER 4
# DOING RIGHT, EVERY DAY

*"The plans of the diligent lead to profit as surely as haste leads to poverty."*
— Proverbs 21:5 NIV

Consistency was another value my mother embodied. As my Aunt Yolanda used to say, "Your mom was always doing something. She never rested." It's so true. From the time I was a child, my mom was constantly on the go, thinking about the next opportunity, the next hustle, and making sure that we had everything we needed. She had a tireless work ethic, and it was because of her consistency, in everything she did, that we always had food on the table and a roof over our heads.

Growing up, I never realized how difficult things were. In fact, I always thought we were wealthy, even though we weren't. I thought we were the richest kids in the neighborhood because of how well my parents provided for us. But as I got older, I came to understand that while we were well-off in the basic sense—food, clothes, and a safe place to live—my parents were hustling constantly to make ends meet. It wasn't until later that I realized just how much my mother had to do to provide for us, how much sacrifice went into creating the life we had.

Everything she built was a result of consistency, whether it was the work she did in the fields, the restaurant and secondhand store she ran, or the property rentals she juggled. Every job she took on, she approached with the same mindset: Do it right, do it consistently.

She would always constantly talk about her faith and doing the right thing. I don't think I would be faith-related to this day if it wasn't for her taking me to church when I was a little kid and teaching me the Word of God.

As kids, we didn't get the luxury of idle time like other kids. We were always working, always doing chores, always helping with the business. And though it felt like a curse at the time, now, as an adult, I see that she was teaching us the importance of routine, of consistency. She didn't just talk about it—she lived it, and the consistent work ethic she instilled in us was a gift that laid the foundation for much of the success I have today.

One of the most impressive aspects of my mother's work ethic was her ability to think outside the box, especially in the context of her business. For example, when she had a crew working in the fields, she would drop us off to manage the laborers while she went back to town to prepare lunch. But here's the genius part: instead of just letting the laborers fend for themselves, she saw an opportunity. She would prepare burritos and bring them back to the workers for lunch, selling them a hot meal instead of leaving them to find food on their own. It wasn't much, but it was another stream of income.

You see, my mother wasn't just running a one-dimensional business. She thought in terms of recurring revenue. She knew that the workers had to eat, so why not sell them food and drinks, too? Why not make the most of the time they were already spending with her? She also took the opportunity to advertise her secondhand store, helping the workers buy clothes and boots they might need for their families back home.

This ability to diversify, to think beyond the immediate task at hand, was crucial to her success. It wasn't just about doing the job and making money; it was about consistently creating ways to multiple income streams. She understood that in business, if you're too focused on just one area, you limit your potential.

As a businessperson, if you can find ways to create recurring revenue from multiple sources, you're setting yourself up for sustainable success. My mother did just that, taking every opportunity to make the most of her resources, and always thinking of ways to serve others while simultaneously growing her business.

But more than anything, my mother's consistency was about relationships. As mentioned in the last chapter, she was always there for her employees, contractors, and anyone who needed her help. She didn't just hire people—she built relationships. She treated her workers with respect and kindness, offering them opportunities not just for work but for growth. She consistently mentored them, gave them advice, and made sure that when they were in need, they could count on her.

The way she consistently cared for others is what made her a successful businesswoman. She knew that success in business wasn't just about profits—it was about creating bonds, building trust, and always being there for people when they need you. She made sure to create a community around her work, and that sense of community fueled her success.

This idea of consistency—doing, day in and day out—is also reflected in biblical teachings. Proverbs 21:5 says, *"The plans of the diligent lead to profit, as surely as haste leads to poverty."* My mother exemplified this verse. She wasn't hasty. She didn't look for shortcuts. She worked steadily and consistently, and it paid off.

Her consistency in everything she did, whether it was her work, her faith, or her relationships, was what led to her success. It wasn't glamorous, and it wasn't easy, but it was effective. And that's a lesson that anyone can apply. Whether pursuing a career, raising a family, or running a business, consistency in your efforts will always lead to growth and success.

One biblical figure who embodies this kind of consistency is Nehemiah. In the book of Nehemiah, he faced enormous opposition when he set out to rebuild the walls of Jerusalem, which were in ruins. But despite the challenges, Nehemiah remained consistent. He stayed focused on his goal, worked tirelessly, and refused to be deterred by setbacks. Through his consistent effort, he completed the task in just fifty-two days, a feat that would have normally taken years.

Nehemiah's story shows us that with consistency and focus, you can accomplish incredible things. Even when the odds are stacked against you, even when others doubt you, staying consistent in your actions, beliefs, and goals can create lasting success.

Whatever the goal, consistency is the cornerstone of success. From my mother's ability to juggle multiple ventures while caring for her workers, to the way she consistently instilled the values of hard work and faith in me, she showed me that success doesn't come from bursts of effort or luck; it comes from steady, consistent action.

That's what I try to carry into everything I do. Whatever the goal, I show up every day, work hard, and stay true to the principles that got me here. Success isn't about doing something spectacular once in a while—it's about doing the right thing, day after day.

So if you want to succeed in anything, be it building a business or simply improving your life, remember that consistency is key. Stick to the grind, keep pushing forward, and success will follow.

> **Axiom:** BE CONSISTENT.
>
> **Bible Verse:** *"The plans of the diligent lead to profit as surely as haste leads to poverty."*
> — Proverbs 21:5 NIV

# CHAPTER 5
# WORK WAS FIRST

*"You will eat the fruit of your labor;*
*blessings and prosperity will be yours."*
— Psalm 128:2 NIV

From a young age, I learned that hard work was not just something you did—it was who you were. My mother never hired a babysitter. She took us everywhere. As a toddler, I remember waking up before dawn, bundled in blankets, getting ready for the long day ahead. It was still dark outside, and the air was chilly. My mother would start one of several trucks we used to transport laborers to the fields. I'd curl up on the floor by the heater, too young to understand the weight of the journey ahead.

As my mother got everything ready, I would watch her in awe. She had a quiet, steady way of taking charge. In Spanish, she'd whisper, "Shut your eyes, go to sleep." But I could never sleep—too afraid of the dark, and too curious about where we were going. The women who worked with her, many of them immigrants like her, would rest up front as we made our way to the job site. My mother was always in charge, coordinating the crew and making sure everyone was where they needed to be. At one point, she was managing twenty to twenty-five workers, ensuring they were comfortable, safe, and productive.

As a child, I spent more time in the trucks than anywhere else. I'd crawl into the camper or play in the dirt while the workers labored under the blistering Texas sun. There was no shade in the fields—just the relentless heat.

But I learned to adapt, finding refuge underneath the truck to stay cool. And when I was old enough, I worked beside my mother in the fields, learning that the work never stopped. We were always looking for more opportunities, more ways to keep going.

By the time I was five, I was already going on cold calls with my mother. While she didn't speak English, I did. I'd knock on farmers' doors, delivering a simple pitch: "Do you need working hands? If you have crops, we have laborers." It was strange for a child to be doing the talking, but that was life in our family—work wasn't a separate thing; it was woven into every part of life. I would translate for my mom, helping her close deals and bring in the next wave of work.

Summers were also for working. After school, I'd meet my mom, and we'd head straight to the labor camps or the fields. Long, grueling days followed by another long day. The physical toll was immense, but there was no complaining. The work had to be done. Hard work wasn't just how we survived—it was how we thrived. My mother didn't just talk about the American Dream; she lived it every day through the sweat of her brow and the strength of her will.

As a preteen, the work became even harder, and I became more accustomed to it. One task stands out—the cucumber harvest. Imagine a flat, sun-baked field stretching for miles. On either side of a slowly-moving diesel truck, workers lined up, each with two five-gallon buckets. The goal was simple: keep pace with the truck, keep your buckets full, and don't stop. I quickly learned that the earlier you arrived, the better your position would be. The truck didn't wait, and if you weren't fast enough, you'd end up farther from the truck, making the work even harder.

The work was intense. The buckets were heavy, and the heat was relentless. Some people couldn't handle it. I remember an older man, a migrant worker in his sixties, who couldn't continue because of back pain. He was in tears. I was strong enough to take on the extra load, so I swapped rows with him, helping him carry his buckets back to the truck.

By then, I started thinking about my own future. I told myself I wouldn't end up doing this kind of work when I was older. I wanted more—a life where my children wouldn't have to work in the fields. But even as I dreamed of something bigger, I never stopped working hard. That summer, I gave all my earnings to my mother. She didn't pay me directly, but she always made sure I had what I needed—food, clothes, whatever. Through this, I learned the value of earning, not just through wages, but through the act of working together, building a life through sweat and sacrifice.

When I was about fourteen or fifteen years old, I began to take on more responsibility. I started driving a tractor and managing laborers. My mom would send me to the field to check on the work. Once, the landowner gave me the keys to a brand new white truck. The only problem was I didn't know how to drive a stick shift. But I wasn't going to back down. I remembered how my dad had driven a stick shift, and I decided to figure it out.

It wasn't easy. The truck bucked and stalled as I made my way through the dirt fields. But after a few rocky moments, I got the hang of it. I learned to drive the truck on my own, without anyone there to guide me. That experience was one of many where I was challenged and chose to face it head-on. It taught me the importance of courage and self-reliance. I could've said no, handed the keys back, and walked away, but I didn't. I embraced the challenge, and in doing so, I grew.

These experiences weren't just about learning how to work hard—they were about learning to rise to the occasion, to challenge myself, and to never back down from an obstacle.

Yet, the reality of hard work wasn't always easy. I saw the harsh realities of life as a child of immigrants. Sometimes, Border Patrol would show up at the fields, and there was nowhere for the workers to hide. I watched as they lined up, asked for documentation, and, if they were undocumented, were taken away. It was heartbreaking to see, especially knowing that many of them had families depending on them. My mother would plead with Border Patrol officers, asking them to let the workers get paid before they were deported. Sometimes, they were compassionate, but other times they weren't.

Through these experiences, I came to respect the immigrant workers who showed up every day to make a living. Many of them had no formal education and no English skills, but they worked tirelessly to build a better life for their families.

My mother's work ethic, and that of those she employed, shaped who I am today. They taught me that no matter what life throws at you, the key to success is hard work. I don't have a special skill set, and I never went to school for business, but I'll tell you, that's what sets you apart.

So identify your purpose and work hard at it. Don't treat it like a job. For me, it wasn't about having a degree or a fancy title. It was about diving into something, learning it, and mastering it. I started as a minimum-wage worker with zero knowledge of the business I'm in today. But through learning and dedication, I worked my way up. And now? I'm the man who runs the show.

It goes back to passion and purpose. If you love what you do, you'll find a way to make it work. And when you work hard, nothing is impossible.

I've always liked Rory Vaden's "buffalo versus cow" approach.

Picture a storm coming—thunder, lightning, hail, all of it. The cow runs away from the storm, and it keeps running and running. Eventually, it's exhausted, and the storm catches up to it. But the buffalo? The buffalo runs toward the storm because it knows that facing it head-on means passing through it much faster.

I've always been the buffalo. When challenges arise, I don't run from them. I face them head-on. And that's exactly what my mom taught me. From childhood to adulthood, every obstacle was an opportunity to grow and get stronger.

When I was out there in the fields, it wasn't by choice. As a kid, I would have preferred to hang out with my friends or go swimming, but my mom didn't allow it. She made sure I was always with her, and while I resented it at the time, looking back, I'm so grateful. She taught me lessons that no classroom could.

The laborers who worked alongside us in those fields shaped my understanding of what hard work truly is. They sent every penny they made back home. It wasn't glamorous work. But the next time you eat a tomato, remember it did not pick itself.

Witnessing that kind of work ethic made me appreciate the value of hard work, of dedicating yourself to something bigger. It made me appreciate where my food comes from, and it gave me a deeper respect for the people who labor so that others can have a better life.

Psalm 128:2 says, "You will eat the fruit of your labor; blessings and prosperity will be yours." At the end of the day, working hard is the key to success. It's the grind. It's showing up every day, rain or shine, and putting in the effort. If you want to go from famine to fortune, you've got to work hard—and never stop.

---

**Axiom:** WORK HARD.

**Bible Verse:** *"You will eat the fruit of your labor; blessings and prosperity will be yours."*

— Psalm 128:2 NIV

# CHAPTER 6
# DISCIPLINE SHAPED ME

*"No discipline seems pleasant at the time, but painful. Later on, however, it produces a harvest of righteousness and peace for those who have been trained by it."*
— Hebrews 12:11 NIV

As I reflect on my upbringing, one thing stands out: it wasn't a lack of love, but a more consistent emphasis on discipline that shaped my path. As I mentioned in earlier chapters, while we weren't the poorest family, we certainly didn't have much. Yet, my siblings and I never understood we were less fortunate. My parents worked tirelessly to provide for us, always ensuring we had food on the table, a roof over our heads, and a full fridge. They shielded us from the reality of financial struggles, making sure we felt secure, even when we didn't have much.

One thing that defined our household more than anything else wasn't affection in the traditional sense. It wasn't about hugs or words like "I love you"—it was about discipline. There were clear expectations, and my mom ran our home with a level of precision and purpose that felt almost businesslike. She balanced multiple businesses, and I was often entrusted with responsibilities that made me feel more like an adult than a child. Whether I was taking care of the store or collecting rent from tenants, my mom expected me to handle my duties seriously.

This taught me early on that life wasn't about waiting for things to be handed to you—it was about taking responsibility for what you had and working hard to achieve your goals.

Discipline wasn't just something that applied to work. It was a way of life. My dad wasn't a man of many words, but his actions spoke volumes. His relentless work ethic taught me that discipline wasn't just about completing tasks—it was about showing up, day after day, regardless of how you felt. His example instilled in me the belief that no matter what, you never quit.

And while affection wasn't always expressed verbally, there were many moments when I felt it, like the time I was five years old, sitting in the truck as we were riding through the desert with my dad on the way to Mexico. My dad looked at me and called me *mijo*, a term of endearment in Spanish, and asked me to change the station on the CB radio. It was a small gesture, but it meant a lot to me. Another time, when I nearly got hit by a car in Mexico while chasing after him, it was my dad who ran to scoop me up, even as my mom scolded him for not keeping a better eye on me.

As I grew older, I began to understand that love wasn't always about words—it was about actions. My parents may not have expressed their affection the way many would expect, but they showed their love by instilling morals, values, and discipline to work hard and face the world with strength. And it was this discipline, more than anything else, that played a crucial role in shaping who I am today. However, these lessons went beyond the home, and the farther I ventured from it, the more diverse forms of discipline I encountered.

My first- and fifth-grade teacher, Barbara Hicks, understood me in a way that few others did. I wasn't a kid who could just sit still and follow the usual routine. When schoolwork didn't challenge me, I'd get bored and find ways to entertain myself, like organizing the first aid kit. But rather than getting frustrated with me, Mrs. Hicks worked with me. She let me negotiate my own terms for completing assignments, and she never made me feel bad for needing a different approach. She was patient and flexible, and because of her, I learned that discipline didn't have to come in one rigid form. It could be adapted to suit the individual, but the foundation of focus and hard work was always there.

Barbara Hicks & Moses Heredia, Hobbs, NM (2019).

I later visited her years after graduating and brought her a gift to show my appreciation. I also remembered how she gave her son Billy's hand-me-down clothes to my mom's secondhand store, which I ended up wearing. She told me that's when she realized how hard we had it. I never forgot her kindness and the way she believed in me, even when I didn't fully understand it myself. Mrs. Hicks taught me that discipline wasn't about conforming to a mold

—it was about pushing through challenges and never giving up, even when things didn't fit neatly into place.

5th Grade with Mrs. Hicks, Edison Elementary School

"You know," she said, "I can still see Moses in my mind, just like it was yesterday. He left quite an impression. When I think about his upbringing, I think about his mom's work ethic. Moses' success had a lot to do with his mother. She was dedicated and did everything she could for those kids."

Moses Heredia in a three-piece suit

The point is that the theme of discipline was woven into everything I did as a child. My mom was always particular about how I looked. She made sure I was well-groomed and presented myself with pride. Even as a child, I couldn't stand stains on my clothes, and I took pride in looking neat.

As an adult, attention to detail has stuck with me. I find that eighty percent of my suits are three-piece suits, just like the ones my mom dressed me in as a kid.

Ultimately, the lessons I learned about discipline helped shape my character and laid the foundation for the success I enjoy today. It's what made me who I am. My parents might not have shown affection in the traditional sense, but they gave me something far more enduring: the ability to work hard, tell the truth, and stay focused—even when the going gets tough.

As Hebrews 12:11 says, *"No discipline seems pleasant at the time, but painful. Later on, however, it produces a harvest of righteousness and peace for those who have been trained by it."*

I remember working alongside immigrants in the fields, often without a paycheck or reward at the end of the day. It didn't feel pleasant at the time, and there were moments I wondered why I was doing it. But my mom didn't do it to punish me. She did it to teach me something far more important than money—she was teaching me discipline and that nothing worth having comes easily.

When I wanted new Converse shoes or a pair of Nikes, my mom wouldn't hand me the money. She'd buy the shoes, but only after I'd earned them by working hard. At the time, I didn't fully understand why she did it that way. It didn't seem fair. But looking back, I now realize that she was teaching me the value of delayed gratification—the discipline to work for something, even when the reward isn't immediate.

That lesson stayed with me as I grew older. The more I worked, the more I learned about discipline—about earning things with integrity, and about not cutting corners. Mrs. Hicks, too, helped shape this perspective. She accepted that I didn't fit the mold of every other student, and she gave me the freedom to approach my work on my own terms. She once said to me, "You can be anything you want. There's no limit to what you can achieve." At the time, I didn't understand the full weight of her words, but as I grew older, I realized that success isn't about what you have or where you come from. It's about your willingness to believe in yourself, as we discussed in chapter two, and to apply the discipline needed to achieve your goals, as it's the foundation of success.

Now, as I look back, I realize that the rewards of discipline aren't always immediately visible. But as Hebrews 12:11 says, they do come. Discipline might not feel good in the moment, but it produces a harvest of righteousness, peace, and strength. It is what has allowed me to overcome obstacles and achieve the success I've experienced. And it's why, no matter where you are in your journey, I'm confident that if you make discipline a cornerstone of your life, you, too, can accomplish anything you set your mind to. The greatest rewards come not from what you see in the moment, but from what you've been preparing for all along. Discipline shapes your future, and that future can be greater than anything you've ever imagined.

As you read this, I want you to think about your own journey, your own dreams, and the aspirations you hold for your life. No matter where you are right now—whether you're just starting out or you've been at it for years—there's one key thing that can unlock all the doors in your life: discipline. If you've ever wondered what separates those who succeed from those who don't, it comes down to discipline.

The truth is that discipline is in every aspect of life. It starts the moment you open your eyes in the morning. You're alive, and that's something to be grateful for. How disciplined are you in thanking God for that gift? How disciplined are you in setting a positive tone for the day, whether that's through your workout, your diet, your work habits, or how you interact with the people around you? Discipline is about making decisions that align with your goals, even when it feels tough.

As an entrepreneur, you'll face endless challenges, constant pressure, and the temptation to cut corners or take shortcuts. But success never comes from shortcuts. It comes from doing the hard work consistently, even when it doesn't feel pleasant. Like I learned growing up, it wasn't easy, and it didn't feel rewarding at the time. But that discipline, that ability to push through discomfort, taught me the true value of hard work. The effort may seem grueling in the moment, but the rewards are worth it.

Think of discipline as a currency. When I was struggling out there in the fields, I viewed every action as diving into the ocean for treasure. You're underwater, gasping for air, unable to come up for a breath—but you keep diving. Why? Because you know there's something valuable waiting for you if you just keep at it. That's the discipline it takes to succeed. In business, every day is a dive, every task is a treasure hunt, and you have to be willing to dive deep, push through the discomfort, and keep grinding until you find that shining object: a breakthrough, a deal, a success.

But just like with diving, once you find that treasure, you don't stop. You bring it up, take a breath, and dive again. Success isn't a one-time thing; it's a continuous effort. You dive into work, you grind, you take your wins, and you go back for more. You develop the discipline to keep pursuing what you want day in, day out. It's about being persistent. If you can approach every part of your life with that mindset—whether it's your fitness, your work, or your relationships—you'll start to see results.

Moses Heredia, age 12.

I learned this early on in everything I did. I remember being a kid on the football field, and every time I didn't give it my all during practice, I would end up hurt. That's when I realized—you get what you put in. If I wasn't giving one hundred percent, I wasn't going to get the results I wanted. The same goes for your business. If you're not giving it everything you've got, you can't expect to see major progress.

For me, discipline has always been about mastering what I do best. There's no magic formula for success, but there is something that sets those who succeed apart from those who don't: focus. You can't expect to excel in ten different areas at once if you're not putting one hundred percent into each of them. Focus on mastering one thing, then move to the next. It's like building a house—you lay the foundation first, then you start stacking brick by brick. The discipline to focus and build gradually will pay off.

You don't have to be the best at everything from the start. It's not about being perfect. It's about pushing forward, day after day, giving your best, and never quitting.

And when you tie this discipline back to a bigger purpose, whether that's providing for your family, changing your community, or living out your faith, it becomes even more powerful. I'm reminded of King David, one of Israel's greatest kings. As a young shepherd, he learned discipline in the field, protecting his sheep from lions and bears. That discipline prepared him to face Goliath. It gave him the strength to rise up against challenges that seemed impossible. David's discipline made him a king. And just like David, when you apply discipline in your own life, you too can overcome your giants and achieve greatness.

So, to all the entrepreneurs out there, to anyone striving for success, remember that it starts with discipline. You can achieve anything you set your mind to, but you have to be disciplined enough to stay the course. Keep your focus. Keep diving for that treasure. The rewards are out there, and they're waiting for those who are willing to put in the work and remain disciplined. Success isn't a destination—it's a journey, and the discipline you cultivate today will carry you to the heights you've always dreamed of.

---

**Axiom:** BE DISCIPLINED.

**Bible Verse:** *"No discipline seems pleasant at the time, but painful. Later on, however, it produces a harvest of righteousness and peace for those who have been trained by it."* — Hebrews 12:11 NIV

# THE GRIND GOT ME HERE

The grind got me here, but it's definitely not because I had a degree or some natural talent that made me stand out. What got me here was the discipline, the dedication, the work ethic, and the relentless drive to succeed. It's the grind that got me where I am today, and I believe it can get you to your destination—if you're willing to put in the work, physically, mentally, and emotionally—one hundred percent.

And this isn't just about working hard—it's about the right kind of hard work. It all starts with a belief in yourself. If you don't believe in your potential, then none of the grind matters. You have to trust that you're capable of more, even when the odds are against you. I've always believed in myself, even when the world tried to tell me I couldn't make it. My mom instilled that belief in me. She showed me the power of seeing something better than what was right in front of you. She'd take me to Mexico and make sure I understood where we came from, how hard life was, and how we could have ended up. But she also made sure I understood that this wasn't my fate. Believing in myself, even when the odds were stacked against me, was my first step.

But believing in yourself isn't enough. You must also practice compassion. You can't succeed alone; people will always be a part of your journey. On our trips back to Mexico, I saw kids without shoes, without food, and families struggling to survive. These trips taught me that while we weren't living in luxury, we had far more than many, and it was our job to lift others along the way because we're all in this together.

Consistency plays a huge role in this process. Being consistent is the key to transforming hard work into real results. You can't grind hard for a week or a month and expect overnight success. You have to be consistent day in and day out, even when the results aren't immediately visible. Whether it's saving money, building relationships, or improving your skill set, consistency is the bridge that connects effort to outcome. For me, consistency meant showing up every single day, regardless of how I felt or what setbacks I faced. When I was a kid, I worked hard even when there was no reward. I had no paycheck, no recognition—just the knowledge that every ounce of effort I put in was getting me closer to something bigger. Whether it was running fast in P.E. or playing football, I was always consistent in pushing myself to be better. It was about doing the right thing over and over, no matter the outcome.

But consistency alone doesn't get you far without hard work. The grind isn't just about clocking in and out—it's about working hard with intention. Hard work is key to achieving any goal. As I said before, when I was a kid, I worked hard without expecting anything in return. I wasn't getting paid, but I wasn't working for a paycheck—I was working to survive and to learn. When I grew older, I applied that same level of dedication and hard work to everything I did. And even though I wasn't always the best or the fastest, my work ethic set me apart. Hard work is what keeps you going when the road gets rough, and when you want to quit, but you keep pushing through. I remember my mom's example—how hard she worked and how she always found a way to push through difficult circumstances. She showed me that hard work is a choice, even when it feels like you're going nowhere.

Lastly, all of this requires discipline. Discipline is what ties everything together and keeps you on track when the grind gets tough. Without discipline, you'll never stay focused long enough to see the results of your hard work. For me, discipline was learned early on through my upbringing. I was disciplined with my savings, disciplined with my time, and disciplined in my approach to business. I didn't waste a dollar; I saved everything I earned. I remember having adults come to me for money when I was a kid. I wasn't a millionaire—I was just a kid who was taught to save and be disciplined. And that mindset carried into everything I did. It's what allowed me to keep going, even when it seemed like I wasn't getting ahead. Discipline isn't about perfection; it's about staying committed to your goals, staying consistent, and sticking with it, no matter what.

So when I say the grind got me here, I'm not just talking about the financial success or the material things I've gained. I'm talking about everything that came with it: belief in myself, compassion for others, consistency in my work, hard work that never stopped, and the discipline to stay on track. These aren't just isolated principles —they're interconnected. They build on each other and form the foundation of the grind.

Without the grind, I wouldn't be where I am today. Yes, faith is important, but faith alone doesn't lead to success. The grind does. The grind is where it all comes together. It's how you achieve your dreams, how you help others, and how you become the person you were meant to be. The grind gave me faith, discipline, and a purpose. It gave me the strength to push through challenges, the vision to see beyond my circumstances, and the belief that I could be something more.

And now, as I look at where I am, I know it's not just about what I've achieved; it's about the people I've helped along the way. The grind allowed me to give back, to show compassion to others, to create opportunities, and to invest in the future of those around me. It's not just about the things I have; it's about what I can do with those things to help others. That's the true measure of success. When I can look around and see people from all walks of life—people who were once like me, struggling to make ends meet—now achieving their own success because of the grind, that's what truly makes it worth it.

"Here" is not just about wealth or material possessions. Here is about giving, helping, and seeing others rise. It's about living with purpose. This is where the grind has taken me, and that's why I will always say: The grind got me here, where I've had the privilege of watching people who started with nothing use that same grind to build something for themselves. That's what it's all about.

# PART TWO
# GOD IS REAL

# CHAPTER 7
# THE WAKEUP CALL

*"Do not be misled: Bad company corrupts good character."*
— Corinthians 15:33 NIV

When I was in high school in Hobbs, New Mexico, I was a sophomore, just starting to get into drinking, partying, and hanging out with my friends. At that point, I was still an athlete, but I was starting to drift into the lifestyle of the "popular kids." We would go out, have fun, and enjoy ourselves.

I remember, at sixteen years old, being in the middle of a night out, coming home and doing my homework while still buzzed from the alcohol. I'd be doing my algebra and assignments, but my focus was scattered.

At the time, I had a close-knit group of friends, many of whom played football with me. We did everything together—ate together, worked together, spent a lot of time at each other's houses. This tight bond was built from years of shared experiences, like fishing, hunting, and just hanging out in our small town. If one of us had a chore to do, we'd call each other up and go to help out just so we could spend more time together.

But despite the camaraderie, I began to notice a dangerous trend. Hobbs was a small town with very little opportunity. The population was only around fourteen thousand, and there wasn't much to do besides get into trouble.

One night, I was driving around town in my parents' pickup truck with a keg of beer in the back, hanging out with my friends. I wasn't even old enough to drive legally, and sure enough, we got pulled over by the police. The officer took my information and told me he'd follow me home to speak with my parents. But instead of feeling regret, the next day, I took the keg, put it back in the truck, and drove off to the next party.

This was just the beginning. I started getting into fistfights, acting out at school, and rebelling against everything I had been raised to believe. I was pushing all the right values aside—until God gave me a wake-up call.

Again, I got picked up by the cops for underage drinking. I was embarrassed and ashamed as I was dropped off at my house. My mother asked if I had been drinking. I lied, saying no, and walked quickly to my room to avoid her gaze. But the next morning, I couldn't escape the shame. I felt the weight of all my bad decisions —all at once. I had disappointed my parents, who had worked so hard to give me a better life. I knew that I was on a path to destruction.

That was the turning point for me—the moment I realized I needed to change. I knew that if I wanted to be successful, I had to get out of Hobbs. But even then, I didn't know how to make that happen. So, I prayed for guidance, and once again, God answered.

I called my older brothers, Rigo and Rafael Heredia, who were already living in California. I didn't ask for permission or share all the details—I simply told them that I was coming, and months later, I had saved up enough money from working in the fields to buy a one-way ticket. Leaving Hobbs was the hardest decision I ever made, but it was also the best. And it was God's wisdom that gave me the clarity to make the right choice. Without Him, I wouldn't have had the strength to leave and build a better life, and I realized then the importance of trusting Him, even when the stakes are high.

This season of my life taught me the importance of making wise decisions, even when they are hard. As the Bible says in 1 Corinthians 15:33, "Bad company corrupts good character." You have the power to choose your path, but you need wisdom to make the right choices.

This is especially relevant for entrepreneurs and anyone seeking success. You must surround yourself with people who uplift you, who push you to grow and do better. If you find yourself in a negative environment, it will only drag you down. Whether it's your social circle or your work environment, it plays a significant role in your success.

In my case, leaving Hobbs was a step toward a better future. It wasn't easy, but it was necessary. The grind wasn't just about working hard—it was about making the right choices, the most important being to leave that environment to build something better for myself and my family.

At the end of the day, it's about the ability to recognize when it's time to change direction, and most importantly, it's about faith. Everyone has a choice. And for me, that choice was to move forward with a better plan, a better mindset, and the faith that I could achieve something greater than I could have ever imagined.

---

**Axiom:** STAY AWAY FROM SMALL-MINDED PEOPLE.

**Bible Verse:** *"Do not be misled: Bad company corrupts good character."*

— Corinthians 15:33 NIV

## CHAPTER 8
## A ONE-WAY TICKET TO CALIFORNIA

*"Then Peter called to him, 'Lord, if it's really you, tell me to come to you, walking on the water.' 'Yes, come,' Jesus said. So Peter went over the side of the boat and walked on the water toward Jesus."*
— Matthew 14:28–29 NLT

As I mentioned in the previous chapter, when I was sixteen years old, I made the decision to leave home. Not my family, but the town itself—the environment that I knew was holding me back. I called my older brother, Rafael, who was living in California, and told him I needed to come stay with him. After saving up enough money, I bought a one-way ticket on the Greyhound, and that was that.

I remember the day I left Hobbs. It was in the middle of my junior year, and it was also my seventeenth birthday. My sister Cenia and my mom drove me to the bus station. All I had with me was a small suitcase and a backpack. I'll never forget the image of my mom standing there, crying, watching me leave. She was with my sister, and I waved to them as the bus pulled away. Before I left, I told them I'd be back, truly believing I'd return soon. I just wanted the chance to finish high school, and I didn't think much beyond that at the time. But leaving wasn't easy. It hurt to leave my mom behind, even though she didn't know the full extent of why I was going. She didn't know about my drinking or my slipping grades. But despite everything, she supported me. She gave me her blessing from the beginning. She never once said, "Don't go." She simply said, "The decision is yours." My dad, too, gave me his blessing.

When I arrived in California, it wasn't easy. I was homesick for months. There were many times I thought about going back, but I knew God had brought me there for a reason, and who was I to disobey an answered prayer? I had to trust that He had a plan for me, and eventually, I settled in.

I made friends, started dating, and stopped drinking. My grades improved. I stayed focused. I worked out regularly. I spent most of my time hitting the books, and before I knew it, I had accumulated more credits than I needed to graduate. I faced every challenge head-on. Without the distractions I had back in Hobbs, I was able to give one hundred percent to everything I did.

Senior year, I transferred to Alta Loma High School, and it turned out to be one of the best years of my life. I went to all the school dances, including prom. I went to the football games. It was a completely different experience from what I had in Hobbs. The people were different, the culture was richer, and the town was safer. For the first time in my life, I felt at peace.

In 1993, I graduated high school. At that point, thanks to the new sense of direction I had found, I was already set on going to college that fall. I started looking for jobs I could take while I was there. I considered joining the Marines or pursuing a career in law enforcement. I had taken various criminal justice courses and completed a law enforcement academy course, so I felt confident I could succeed in either path. But instead, I made a decision that would change the course of my life: I took a full-time job with a credit card processing company.

It was that decision, along with all the others that came before it, that set the stage for everything that came after.

If you're feeling like you've hit a dead end, stuck in a bad situation with no one encouraging you to do better, you have to make a choice. You have to take action, even if it means reevaluating your environment.

Your environment plays a crucial role in shaping who you are and where you'll go. It can either push you forward or hold you back. For me, the decision to leave Hobbs wasn't just about leaving my family or my home. It was about leaving an environment that wasn't helping me grow. Yes, it was hard. But sometimes, to reach your true potential, you have to go through periods of discomfort and loneliness. You have to be willing to step out, even when you feel uncertain or unprepared. For me, that meant heading to California with no friends, no routine, and no real support system. But I did it because I knew that if I stayed where I was, I would stay stuck.

Making that hard choice to step out and pursue something better wasn't easy, but it was necessary. And the same is true for you. If you're stuck in a place that's holding you back, you have to take action. It's up to you to get on the bus. You must bet on yourself, trust that you can change, stay focused, and take that first step toward a better future.

One of the biggest distractions I see, especially amongst entrepreneurs and goal-driven people, is what I call "shiny ball syndrome." It's when something new, exciting, or promising catches your eye, and you get distracted by it. You chase that shiny object, only to have another one pop up, pulling your attention away again. Next thing you know, you're all over the place, losing sight of the things that truly matter.

This is where focus comes in. You must block out distractions and prioritize the things that are actually going to get you closer to your goals. Staying focused means tuning out the noise and putting your energy into what truly matters—your purpose, the things that will move you forward.

I could have spent my entire life grinding in the cotton fields of Hobbs, but that wasn't my purpose. That's the difference between being busy and being productive. You can work all day long and still not get anywhere if you're focused on the wrong things.

To get where you want to go, you need to stay locked in on your goals. Focus on what matters—your health, your career, your faith. Focus on what's going to make you better, put you in the right environment, and bring you closer to your dreams. And when you start something, finish it. Success doesn't come from half-hearted effort. It comes from consistent, focused work.

Now, let me take a moment to talk about faith. There will be moments when you feel lost or uncertain, but know this: God has a plan for you. Even when you can't see the way forward, He's always there—guiding, directing, and supporting you, even in the toughest of times. I've experienced it firsthand. When I felt stuck or unsure of my purpose, I turned to God, and He opened doors I never imagined.

There's a passage in the Gospel of Matthew that speaks to me during moments of doubt or uncertainty. In this passage, after a long day of teaching, Jesus sends His disciples ahead of Him across the Sea of Galilee while He goes up to a mountain to pray. The disciples, in a boat, are battling against strong winds and rough waves, and they're making little progress. It's late at night, and they're exhausted. Then something incredible happens. The passage says:

> *"Immediately after this, Jesus insisted that his disciples get back into the boat and cross to the other side of the lake, while he sent the people home. After sending them home, he went up into the hills by himself to pray. Night fell while he was there alone. Meanwhile, the disciples were in trouble far away from land, for a strong*

*wind had risen, and they were fighting heavy waves. About three o'clock in the morning, Jesus came toward them, walking on the water. When the disciples saw him walking on the water, they were terrified. In their fear, they cried out, 'It's a ghost!' But Jesus spoke to them at once. 'Don't be afraid,' he said. 'Take courage. I am here!' Then Peter called to him, 'Lord, if it's really you, tell me to come to you, walking on the water.' 'Yes, come,' Jesus said. So Peter went over the side of the boat and walked on the water toward Jesus."*

This moment is powerful because it demonstrates the essence of focus and faith. Peter didn't know how he would walk on water, but he knew that if Jesus called him, he would be able to do it. His focus was on Jesus, not the storm, not the waves, not the fear around him. He didn't hesitate when he took that first step.

We all face storms in our lives. We all have moments when the wind seems to be against us, when things don't seem to be going our way, when we're battling discouragement or loneliness. But if we keep our focus on the right thing—on God's calling, on our purpose—He will guide us through.

Peter didn't walk on water because he was a great swimmer or because he was naturally skilled at walking on water. He walked on water because he kept his eyes on Jesus and trusted Him completely. When he took his focus off of Jesus and instead focused on the storm, he began to sink, but when he cried out, Jesus reached out His hand and saved him.

Just like Peter, when you step out, the storms of life might still be there, but you have to trust that God will hold you up. Keep your focus on Him, and keep moving forward, even if you don't know exactly how things will turn out.

The first step toward your breakthrough is often the hardest. But with focus and a little faith, you can achieve the impossible.

> **Axiom:** STAY FOCUSED.
>
> **Bible Verse:** *"Then Peter called to him, 'Lord, if it's really you, tell me to come to you, walking on the water.' 'Yes, come,' Jesus said. So Peter went over the side of the boat and walked on the water toward Jesus."*
> — Matthew 14:28–29 NLT

## CHAPTER 9
## TO THE BANK, NOT THE BARS

*"Be very careful, then, how you live—not as unwise but as wise, making the most of every opportunity, because the days are evil."*
— Ephesians 5:15 NIV

To back up a little, I want to go back to when I first graduated high school, before I took the job at the credit card processing company. At the time, I had no job and wasn't sure what I wanted to do. It was 1994, and the internet was nothing like it is now. There weren't job boards to scroll through. Back then, if you were looking for work, you went to the unemployment office.

My friend Anthony Araguz and I were in the same boat. We just got out of high school, and we needed to figure out how to make money. We decided to head over to the unemployment office in Pomona, California, on Holt Street, to see what was available.

I remember walking into that office—it had the same sterile feel as a DMV. You'd take a number, wait to be called, then sit down with someone who asked about your background and what kind of job you were looking for.

At the time, Anthony and I were just teenagers, so our experience was pretty limited. I had worked for my family, but didn't have any official job history or documents to show for it. Still, the woman at the desk was nice enough to hand us a list of job openings. Most of the jobs listed were fast food or other entry-level positions—jobs we were qualified for, paying around $4.25 an hour.

But then I saw something that stood out—a telemarketing position for a bank processor. I didn't know much about telemarketing, and I was still toying with the idea of going into law enforcement, but I needed to start earning income. It was an opportunity, and I decided to take advantage of it.

The lady behind the desk told me they were hiring and suggested I go to fill out an application. So the next day, I showed up at the office. The manager greeted me, handed me an application, and after I filled it out, he took a quick look at it and asked, "Can you start tomorrow?" No interview, no grilling questions. Just a handshake, and I was hired.

The next day, I walked into the office for my first official day. I was handed a Yellow Pages phone book, a phone, and assigned a cubicle. The task? To call everyone in the phone book and make appointments for someone to talk to them about credit card services.

I had no clue what I was doing. But I stuck with it. Hour after hour, I made call after call. It wasn't easy. But finally, after about six hours of calling, someone showed interest in what I was offering. I booked the appointment, and I remember feeling relieved. I thought, "I'm not doing so bad."

As the days went on, I got better at it. I became more confident. And by the third week, I was promoted to telemarketing manager, tasked with managing a team of ten people.

Then, about two months into the job, something happened that would change the course of my career. An auto glass shop owner called. He wanted credit card services for his business, but he didn't speak much English. He needed someone bilingual to visit him in person. I booked the appointment and told my manager, but he brushed it off. "We don't have anyone who speaks Spanish," he said, "just keep making calls."

But here's the thing: I didn't wait for permission. I recognized an opportunity, so without telling my manager, I drove an hour to Simi Valley, met the owner, and after talking with him, I closed the deal. I sold him on the service, and that sale earned me nearly one thousand dollars—my first real success in sales. It wasn't just the money that mattered; it was the realization that this was something I could really do. That moment confirmed my passion for sales. It opened my eyes to the possibilities, to recognizing opportunity, how much you could earn through hard work, and how much opportunity was out there if you said yes to the grind.

By 1994, I became one of the top sales agents for the company in California. And thank God for that, because by then, I had responsibilities. I had bills to pay, for which I couldn't rely on my parents. I had to hustle.

Moses Heredia in 1993 with a 1979 Honda Accord

I remember my friends asking, "Why don't we see you at the bar?" And I would joke, "Why don't I see you at the bank depositing checks?" While they were out partying, I was building my future. While their parents were paying for their car and school, I didn't have time or the luxury of celebrating. Besides, there was nothing to celebrate because I hadn't accomplished anything yet. I was still driving my old 1979 Honda Accord. I was focused, disciplined, and making sacrifices. But I wasn't doing it for anyone else. I was doing it for myself, for my future. This was my shot, and I wasn't going to waste it.

Looking back, there's a clear lesson here: Recognize the opportunities in front of you, even when you don't fully understand them. Step into the unknown and be willing to face the challenges that come with it.

The reality is that we all have to make choices. And every choice counts. If I had said no to that telemarketing job, or if I had dismissed that client because it wasn't "in my job description," I would have missed out on everything that followed. That first sale wouldn't have happened. My career wouldn't have taken off. I wouldn't be where I am today.

As entrepreneurs, we're often faced with opportunities—some big, some small. And the ones who succeed are the ones who don't wait for the perfect moment or for someone else to make the decision for them. They take action. They seize opportunities, even when they don't have all the answers. They step into the unknown, knowing that it's part of the journey.

But it's not just about saying yes to opportunity; it's also about saying yes to yourself. The discipline to follow through, the grit to push through the hard times, and the patience to keep going when things get tough—that's what makes the difference.

I could have easily been distracted. I could have chased the fun stuff—partying, taking the easy route. But I left Hobbs because I knew that wasn't the path for me. I knew that those distractions would keep me from my goal. Instead, I chose to stay focused. I chose the grind. And that choice paid off.

Sacrifice matters. It's the sacrifices you make today that set you up for success tomorrow. Everything has an expiration date, even our lives. So, if you don't seek that opportunity and conquer it today, it's going to affect you three months, six months, a year from now. The discipline to stay focused, to keep working even when it's hard, will pay off in the long run. The friends who partied while I was working? Many of them still regret not starting their careers earlier. But I didn't waste time. I said yes to the opportunities, and I committed to my goals.

There is no tomorrow. The sooner you start, the better off you'll be. You may not see the rewards immediately, but every step you take today is building your future. What you do today will impact the next three months, the next year. So, don't wait. Don't put it off. Say yes to the grind. Say yes to your future.

As Ephesians 5:15 says, *"Be very careful, then, how you live. Not as unwise, but as wise, making the most of every opportunity, because the days are evil."*

The opportunities are there, right in front of you. What you do with them today will determine where you are tomorrow. So, don't wait for the perfect moment. Don't wait for someone else to tell you it's time. Take the opportunity. Say yes.

And don't just say yes to opportunities—say yes to yourself. Because when you do, everything else will fall into place.

---

**Axiom:** RECOGNIZE YOUR OPPORTUNITIES.

**Bible Verse:** *"Be very careful, then, how you live—not as unwise but as wise, making the most of every opportunity, because the days are evil."*
— Ephesians 5:15 NIV

# CHAPTER 10
# DETERMINATION BEFORE DEFEAT

*"But he said to me, 'My grace is sufficient for you, for my power is made perfect in weakness.' Therefore, I will boast all the more gladly about my weaknesses so that Christ's power may rest on me."*
— 2 Corinthians 12:9 NIV

About six months into my job at the credit card processing company, I got into a car accident. After a long day at the office, I was driving home on the interstate. But everything after that gets a bit blurry.

I remember hearing a loud screeching noise, then glancing at the rearview mirror. Then, suddenly, I was waking up, facing incoming traffic. Smoke was filling the car, the steering wheel was broken, and the mirror I had just looked into was gone. My windshield was cracked, and my stereo had popped out. The car was a mess inside, and the outside was smashed from the impact. Meanwhile, cars continued to pass by—tens of them—without slowing down or stopping to help, as if nothing had happened. I was dazed and disoriented, but I wasn't about to wait for someone else to take action. I climbed out of the wreckage, checked my body, and realized I could still move. My face was cut, but the bleeding was minor. My legs and back were sore, but I could walk. At that moment, I just began to thank God for being alive. All I could do then was focus on my next move.

First, I was hit with a cold reality: I couldn't afford a new car. I was only nineteen years old, had no credit to speak of, and no savings. And the car was just the start of my problems. I was on commission-only pay at the time, so if I couldn't get to work, I couldn't make money. I couldn't collect unemployment or any kind of assistance. I didn't want to bother my parents either, so I didn't call them for help. I knew I had to do this on my own.

So, I got creative. I called friends to get rides to work and appointments. I took the MetroLink, borrowed bikes, and hustled in every way I could. In Southern California, you can't get to any destination without transportation.

That struggle lasted for months. I was always on the grind to save up every penny to work to replace it. There were days when I couldn't pay my electric bill. I borrowed an extension cord from a neighbor just to have light to get ready for bed. I went without hot water, taking cold showers in the winter, just to keep pushing through. At one point, my trash bill got so high that I had to ask a neighbor if I could put my trash bins with theirs. As time went on, the trash guys stopped picking it up, so I had my trash pile up in my backyard, and my friend Hector Meneses would come by in his blue pickup truck to pick it up and throw it away in trash bins in the area. Sometimes, I even had to go to fast food restaurants and take napkins and toilet paper from the restroom just to make due.

And though I may not have been able to afford a nice meal, hot showers, or even basic necessities like toilet paper or napkins, I wasn't going to lose my home. I prioritized the essentials, and I kept working. I lived with urgency, and I didn't feel sorry for myself. I couldn't wait for things to improve—I had to take action, and make the most of every single day. It wasn't glamorous, but it was survival.

But it wasn't just survival that kept me going; it was my faith. I remember one night, after everything seemed to be falling apart, I got on my knees and I prayed to Him. Tears were coming down my face, and all I could hear was, *"Don't give up."* I prayed for strength, for guidance, and for the courage to keep going. I had left my small hometown to come to California for a better life, but now, it felt like the doors were closing in on me. I felt like I was running out of options, but in that moment, I felt God's presence. The Apostle Paul encouraged the church in 2 Corinthians 12:9—*"But he said to me, 'My grace is sufficient for you, for my power is made perfect in weakness.' Therefore, I will boast all the more gladly about my weaknesses so that Christ's power may rest on me."*

When I was at my weakest, when it felt like I couldn't keep going, God's grace was enough. His power is made perfect in our weakness. I now realize that my struggle wasn't in vain—it was shaping me into someone stronger, more determined, and more resilient.

Every day, I woke up with a fire in my heart, knowing that tomorrow is never promised, and I had to take advantage of the day at hand. I remember thanking God every time I landed a deal, and the tears of joy that would come when I closed a sale, because it was a victory. A victory that meant I was still moving forward.

Today, I still live with that same urgency. Your struggles don't define you—they shape you. All you have to do is start.

That's how I've survived, how I've thrived, and how I continue to move forward, no matter what life throws at me. I don't look at what I have—I look at what I can do. How can I make a difference today? How can I help others? How can I be better than I was yesterday?

So, start today. Don't feel sorry for yourself. Take action. Keep moving forward. And trust that God's grace will carry you through. There's so much power in grace.

> **Axiom:** DON'T FEEL SORRY FOR YOURSELF.
>
> **Bible Verse:** *"But he said to me, 'My grace is sufficient for you, for my power is made perfect in weakness.' Therefore, I will boast all the more gladly about my weaknesses so that Christ's power may rest on me."*
> — 2 Corinthians 12:9 NIV

# CHAPTER 11
# HARD WORK PAYS OFF

*"Do you see a man skilled in his work? He will stand before kings; he will not stand before obscure men."*
— Proverbs 22:29 NIV

As mentioned in the last chapter, after the accident, I had to grind harder than ever. Even though I was without transportation and was using what little I had to cover the basic necessities, it never stopped me from pushing to be the best at my craft.

Soon, I started to see the light at the end of the tunnel. My bills were getting paid, and I could afford to eat—something I didn't always have the luxury of before. By 1994, I was even recognized as the top sales rep, and then again in 1995.

In 1996, I hit another milestone: I was able to purchase a used car, a 1987 Honda CRX. I remember the first night I got it, I was ecstatic and so worried someone would steal it that I parked it sideways on my driveway. In my eyes, it might as well have been a

Rolls-Royce. I loved that car, and I appreciated it even more because of everything I'd been through to get to that point.

Driving that car was more than just a mode of transportation—it represented freedom. No longer did I have to rely on others for rides. The simple fact that I had my own car pushed me into overdrive. I woke up earlier, worked longer hours, and had the flexibility to travel further to reach more clients. The world suddenly felt wide open. I had complete control over my schedule, and nothing felt more empowering than that.

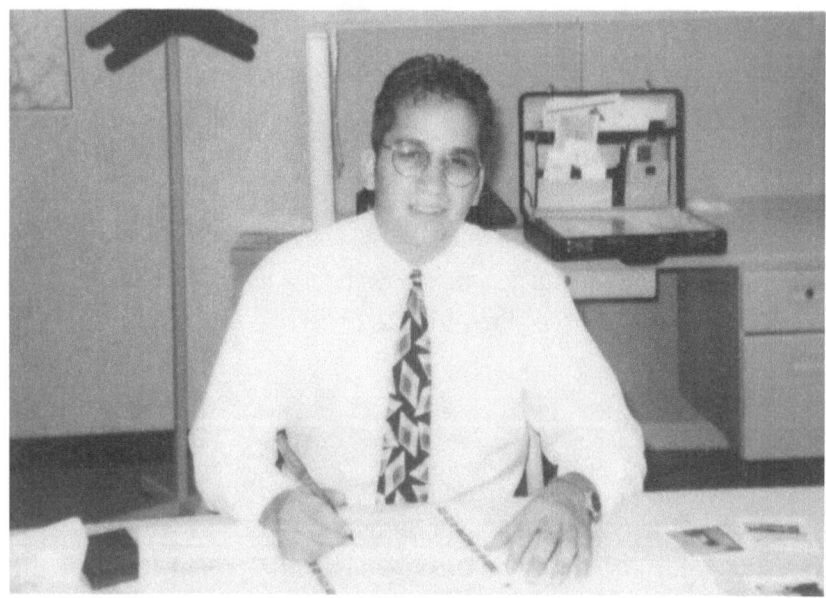

Moses Heredia – Sales Representative, 1994

I was doing so well that the owner of my company at the time, National Processing Company, took notice. He told me he was keeping an eye on my progress, with the potential for promotion. It was exactly what I wanted.

Moses Heredia – Territory Manager, 1997

In 1997, at just twenty-two years old, I was promoted to territory manager for Southern California and was asked to open my own branch there. It didn't take long before I was promoted again to district manager, and then again to regional manager, tasked with leading seven offices and one hundred employees and bringing the offices up to company standards.

It was a lot of pressure, but I knew how to handle it, and it wasn't long before my efforts were recognized in a big way: I received awards and was even flown out to different parts of the country for meetings and celebrations. I was the only territory manager in the entire company who was consistently invited to present my business plan, showcasing how I was able to hit my targets and close deals.

People admired my discipline, and I always made sure to give credit to my mother for teaching me everything I knew about business. Her lessons, her work ethic—those were the foundation of my success.

After ten years holding various positions within the company, I received an offer to become the vice president of sales. It was a huge opportunity, but I turned it down. I knew that it was time for a change, a new venture where I could continue teaching people the skills I had developed and help them achieve the same level of success.

Leaving that position to start my own business was one of the best decisions I've ever made. Today, I'm still in touch with the previous owners of the company, and we catch up at industry conventions. But at the end of the day, taking that risk to move on and create something of my own has been one of the greatest rewards of my career. And it goes to show—sometimes, the biggest risks lead to the biggest rewards.

The hustle for me was an obsession to succeed. I was driven to be the best at everything I did, and I was fiercely competitive. I didn't rely on anyone to get ahead—I had to do it for myself. Independence was something my mom taught me from a young age, and that mindset became a core part of my identity. I was self-taught, constantly pushing myself to be better, to learn more, and to grow faster than the competition.

Featured in First Alliance Newsletter – June 1997

When I started in sales at nineteen years old, I had no formal training. No one gave me a guidebook. So, I created my own. I recorded my meetings, listened to them, critiqued myself, and made adjustments. Day in, day out. I would replay the tapes, analyze every interaction, and ask myself, "How can I get better?" I was my own toughest critic, always looking for ways to improve.

What I quickly realized was that knowledge is power. If you want to be great at something, you need to know more than anyone else—more than your competitors, more than your colleagues. You have to be the expert. I taught myself everything I could about the products and services I was offering, because mastery is what separates the best from the rest.

During the years when my friends were out partying, I was in grind mode. While they were at the bars, I was at the bank. Sure, they laughed and asked why I didn't come out, but I didn't mind. I didn't need a weekend out—I needed to build something that would last. I wasn't interested in the temporary fun they were having. I was building an empire, and that meant sacrifices. I missed weddings, birthdays, anniversaries, but I don't regret any of it. There will always be time for vacations, parties, and breaks—but you can't get back your youth. I made sure I burned the candle at both ends, working relentlessly to create something bigger than myself.

This mindset wasn't just about doing what I loved—it was about mastering what I loved, and to master your passion, you have to take full responsibility for it. I didn't just want to be good at a few aspects of business—I wanted to be the best in all of them. Mastering your craft means taking control of every detail. You can't just dip your toe in and expect to stand out. You have to dive in fully and own every aspect of what you do.

For me, that meant handling everything—from customer support to sales, to tech, and beyond. I didn't want to be someone who had to rely on others to handle the parts I didn't want to deal with. I wanted to know every facet of my business, so no one could ever surpass me.

At the end of the day, mastering your passion requires discipline, dedication, and a willingness to take risks. And if you do it right, it creates a ripple effect. When you master your passion, you build something bigger—something that can help others. Look at what I was able to achieve.

Proverbs 22:29 says, *"Do you see a man skilled in his work? He will stand before kings; he will not stand before obscure men."* It speaks to the idea that excellence, hard work, and mastery in your field don't just get noticed—they propel you to the highest levels. And that is exactly what I've experienced.

David Gomez—CEO, Clean Energy Solutions

*David met Moses through a high school friend, Hector Meneses, while Moses was working his first commission-only sales job after high school.*

"Moses's discipline is unmatched, and it's been that way since the early days. Back when we were working in the same office complex, he was putting in sixty- to seventy-hour weeks like it was no big deal. Even if it was a holiday or weekend, he just never took days off. He's always had this relentless drive, and it's not just in his work. I remember him selling credit card machines, knocking on doors, facing rejection over and over, but he didn't stop. But what really sets him apart is his humility. He's not just a hard worker; he's someone who genuinely connects with people. I've seen him walk into restaurants where he knows everyone—the waiters, the busboys, the owners—by name.

Once, at the Ritz in Laguna, the waiter brought out homemade salsa, just because of the bond he had with the staff. That's not something you see from most successful people. Moses doesn't act like he's above anyone; he's just as comfortable talking to the carwash guys at his house as he is with a CEO. His humility, combined with his discipline, is what makes him so special."

When I first entered the workforce, I didn't have a clear blueprint for success, but I knew one thing: I had to work hard and become the best at what I did. I was determined to prove myself, and over the years, my work ethic and dedication paid off in ways I could never have predicted.

At the beginning of my career, I worked tirelessly, refining my skills, learning from every interaction, and pushing myself to go beyond my limits. Early on, I began to see how the Bible verse came to life for me. My hard work and discipline led me from top salesman to territory manager, and then to district and regional manager. But I didn't get there by just working hard—I was driven by a higher purpose.

**God, Goals, Grind, and Global Impact.** These four principles have been the foundation of my journey and the driving force behind my success. They are the core message of this book, and the main lesson I hope you take away from it. These principles have shaped my life, and I believe they can guide and inform your own path to success as well.

First and foremost, God was always with me. I would pray for wisdom and understanding in my work, and for strength to face the challenges ahead. I believe that Matthew 7:7—"*Ask and it will be given to you; seek and you will find; knock and the door will be opened to you*"—truly embodies the way I approached life and work. Every step of the way, I would pray for God to open doors for me, and He did.

From a young age, I was goal-oriented. I vividly remember plastering my cubicle with pictures of exotic cars and other material goals I wanted to achieve. But it wasn't just about the cars—it was about having a vision, setting goals, and keeping them in front of me every day. Out of sight, out of mind is a true saying. If you don't keep your goals visible and in focus, they fade away.

As I started reaching those goals, I would set bigger ones. I remember one goal was to own a particular car. After I reached that goal, I realized I didn't even want the car anymore, so I crossed it off the list. It wasn't about the object itself—it was about the growth and the journey of achieving what I set my mind to.

Then came the grind—the relentless pursuit of success. The

hustle was in my blood. I treated every job I had like it was my own company, always pushing forward. I would work long hours, often sacrificing personal time, because I knew that the grind was necessary for success.

Let's back up to a time before I received any sort of advancement at the credit card processing company. I was twenty-two years old, but after years of hard work and dedication, I was told I was being considered for a new role. However, after much anticipation, the company ultimately decided to delay the promotion. They said I was "too green" and not ready for such a big responsibility. I was devastated. I had been putting in the work, and I was confident in my abilities, so this delay felt like a personal blow.

In my frustration, I packed up my office, flipped everything on my desk, and walked out. I wasn't sure if I was quitting or if they were going to fire me, but I knew one thing: I had to make a choice. That day was a turning point for me. I didn't let anger define me for long. Instead, I decided to prove them wrong. When they called me to come back, I did. And I worked even harder to demonstrate my capabilities.

I was promoted a few months later, but it wasn't an easy road. I wasn't just handed success—I earned it through hard work, dedication, and a relentless pursuit of excellence. By the time I became a territory manager, I had already built a reputation as one of the top performers in the company.

As I moved up the ranks, from territory manager to district manager to regional manager, my responsibility grew, and my goals expanded. But each step was a reflection of the same core principles.

One of the defining moments of my career came when I was twenty-three. I was invited to a company meeting, where one of the owners, who had been watching me closely, gave me a special gift —stock in the company. He told me to write a check for a certain amount, and he would give me equity. At the time, I didn't fully understand the significance of what he was offering, but I realized years later that he was giving me not just stock, but a partnership in the company. It was his way of showing that he believed in me and my potential, even at such a young age.

That moment was a clear sign that my hard work had not only earned me promotions but had positioned me for greater leadership and influence. And it didn't stop there. As I continued to rise, I developed a deep sense of responsibility—not only for my own success but for helping others succeed as well. I learned how to develop people. I didn't just want to be the best; I wanted to build the best teams. My mother was a huge influence in teaching me the importance of relationships, integrity, and structure in business. She might not have had a formal business education, but she had street smarts and a deep understanding of how to build relationships and businesses. I learned from her that business is really simple: don't lie, cheat, or steal, and build good relationships. No matter how successful I became, I knew I couldn't do it alone. In the same way that Michael Jordan needed his teammates or Tom Brady needed his offensive line, I needed my team to succeed. I always believed that success was about working together, relying on each other, and building a team that would push me to new heights.

In my career, I've been fortunate to be the only Latino in many of the senior management meetings. I was invited to sit at the table with executives because I had proven that I was capable of managing the largest offices, developing strong relationships with clients, and achieving results. I was the best at what I did—not because of luck, but because I had built a well-oiled machine of a team, driven by hard work and ethical business practices.

Even after ten years with the company, I never stopped grinding. I worked through illness, I traveled constantly, and I treated the company as if it were my own. My work ethic was non-negotiable. And that same mindset is what allowed me to take over non-performing offices and turn them around. I would get out in the field, show my team how to sell, how to build relationships, and how to close deals. I wasn't just a leader from the top—I led by example.

And this is where global impact came into play. I didn't want to just make money—I wanted to make a lasting difference. I always believed in serving others, whether it was clients, vendors, or the communities we worked with. I named my company Global Processing Systems because I wanted everything I did to have a ripple effect that would impact lives and businesses on a broader scale.

As I built my company, I kept the values of integrity and transparency at the forefront. We are known for answering the phone, for being accessible to our clients, and for doing what we said we would do. I built this company not for short-term profit, but for long-term impact. We've been in business for over twenty-one years, and we continue to grow because of the foundation we've built: trust, hard work, and a relentless pursuit to be the best in the business.

---

**Axiom:** MASTER YOUR PASSION.

**Bible Verse:** *"Do you see a man skilled in his work? He will stand before kings; he will not stand before obscure men."*
— Proverbs 22:29 NIV

## CHAPTER 12
## PAYING IT FORWARD

*"Jesus looked at them and said, 'With man this is impossible, but with God all things are possible.'"*
— Matthew 19:26 NIV

After I left Hobbs, I never went back. I didn't want to return empty-handed. I knew it would take time—after the car accident, as I mentioned in earlier chapters, there was a period when I couldn't even afford food—but I was determined that when I went back, I would have a gift for my mom. It took six years before I felt I was ready.

During that time, I started planning. My mom never really believed in bank accounts, so I decided to withdraw a large sum of cash and take that with me. After a road trip through the Southwest, visiting extended family along the way, I finally pulled up to the house where I was born and raised. To my shock, it was vacant and boarded up. I couldn't believe it. There had to be some mistake.

I called my sister, still sitting in the driveway, and asked, "What's going on? I'm here, where's Mom? What's happening?" That's when I found out the house had been foreclosed on and repossessed. My mom, not wanting to worry me, had never told me what was going on. I understood, though. I had done the same thing in the past, trying to shield her from my struggles.

After getting her new address, I drove over to see her. She was renting a place in poor condition, and when I saw her, grey-haired and wrinkled, I realized just how much older she had become in those six years. I had hoped to return to her the same way I left her, but that was far from the case.

Moses Heredia Sr., Moses Heredia Jr., and Elestina Heredia – Brick House, 1998

Before I arrived, I had told my parents that I was going to give them some money, but when I saw the condition of things, I realized that wasn't enough. What I needed to do was find her a better place to live. I started driving around, searching for houses in decent neighborhoods. I wanted something nice for her, something that reflected her worth. She deserved the best.

I eventually found a house that caught my eye. It was a brick home—a rare sight in an area known for poverty. Growing up there, I knew that only the wealthy could afford brick homes. A brick home was a symbol of stability and security.

I didn't show it to my mom right away. Instead, I took my childhood pastor, Sister Arpie Palmer, to see it with me. I wanted her to pray over the house before making any decisions. We didn't go inside; I hadn't yet gotten in touch with the agent. But as we stood outside, Sister Palmer began praying over the house, jumping up and down with excitement. "This is going to be your mom's house," she said. "I can see it. God is going to deliver this house to you."

Sister Arpie Palmer and Moses Heredia

I chuckled, but I also knew she was a woman of faith, and I believed in the power of prayer. I thanked her, took her back home, and started pursuing the house. I contacted the agent, made an offer, and soon, everything was moving forward.

But when I went to the bank to finalize the deal, I was met with frustration. The bank was slow-moving, and I couldn't get anything done. Coming from California, where everything was fast-paced, I couldn't understand why things were moving at such a crawl. So, I took matters into my own hands—literally. I moved the banker out of his desk and got on his computer to print the required paperwork. I was only in town for a few days, and I wasn't going to let this opportunity slip away.

Finally, everything was in place, and I showed the house to my parents before making the final offer. They were ecstatic, and I went ahead and sealed the deal. But I had to return to California; at this time, I was district manager at the credit card processing company, so I left the house in limbo, waiting for everything to go through.

As I got back into the grind of work, I received a call from the lender and real estate agent: they told me I didn't qualify for the loan because they considered me an investor, not a primary resident, due to my property ownership in California. They required an extra down payment that I simply couldn't afford.

I didn't tell anyone about this setback—not my sister, not the church, not anyone. I just quietly tried to figure out what to do next. Then, hours later, my sister called me. Sister Palmer and another pastor were on their way to pray for the house because they knew I was having challenges with the purchase. Again, God proved He was real.

I was overwhelmed with emotion, so I told my sister I'd call her back later. It was amazing how Sister Palmer had not only prophesied that this house would be mine, but that I was facing difficulties with the purchase. She had prayed for everything to align, and I truly believed her prayers would work. Still, I couldn't shake my anxiety—I felt like I had failed my mom. I had no idea how I would come up with the money they were requesting. My bank account was tapped out.

Then, a week later, I received a check in the mail. Apparently, I had hit multiple sales goals for the company, and they sent me an unexpected bonus. I opened the check, and it was astonishing: with this money, I was able to cover the down payment for the house. I had no idea this bonus was coming, and yet it was exactly what I needed.

It felt like divine intervention. God was looking out for me, and with that check, I was able to secure the home I had prayed for. It was a moment that solidified my faith even more, and I knew that no matter how hard things got, I could always rely on God to provide.

That's where Matthew 19:26 comes in. It reminds us that with

God, all things are possible, no matter how impossible they may seem.

In the story of the feeding of the five thousand, Jesus is surrounded by a large crowd of people, and His disciples are worried about how they'll feed everyone. The challenge seems insurmountable. In John 6, Philip says it would take more than half a year's wages just to buy enough bread to feed the crowd. And then Andrew, another disciple, finds a boy with five loaves of barley bread and two fish. But even he wonders aloud, *"How far will this go among so many?"*

But Jesus, knowing that the situation seems impossible to the disciples, takes the loaves and fish, gives thanks, and begins distributing them. Miraculously, everyone eats until they're satisfied. And there's even food left over—twelve baskets full.

This is exactly how I felt when I was trying to buy my mom a house and faced a financial setback. I had no idea how I was going to come up with the extra down payment the bank requested. I had already emptied my savings. But God proved His faithfulness. The bonus check was an answer to prayer, a miracle that allowed me to keep my promise to my mom and change her life for the better.

This message is crucial for entrepreneurs. In business, we face challenges that may seem insurmountable—whether it's a financial hurdle, a setback in growth, or a competitor that seems unbeatable. But the lesson from Jesus' miracle is clear: no obstacle is too great when you trust in God.

I've seen this in my own journey as an entrepreneur, and also in the lives of others who have overcome incredible odds. Take, for example, some of the most successful people in the world. Sylvester Stallone was rejected repeatedly before making it big in Hollywood, Michael Jordan was cut from his high school basketball team, and Oprah Winfrey was told she didn't have what it took to be a television host. These people didn't let obstacles define them. They pushed through—and so can you.

In fact, I've seen miracles in my own business journey as well.

## MOSES HEREDIA

My brother Rafael and I won two championships with two different boxers we managed. One was an underdog who ended up winning the WBC World Champion Belt and backed it up with Fight of the Year; the other boxer won the IBF World Championship.

Rafael Heredia, Francisco Vargas, and Moses Heredia – WBC World Champion, 2015

Francisco Vargas, and Moses Heredia

# FIELDS TO FORTUNE

Moses Heredia, Francisco Vargas, and Rafael Heredia

Moses and Rafael Heredia

We faced a lot of adversity, but we stayed committed to the process. I remember one fight in particular where our boxer was knocked down several times. But I prayed on the sidelines, calling out to Jesus, asking Him for victory if it was His will. And we won. That victory, like so many others, was not just the result of hard work—it was a miracle.

And then there were the times I had the privilege of meeting our current president, Donald J. Trump. I was amazed by his belief in God and his faith, despite all the challenges he faced—challenges that included multiple assassination attempts. His faith, like mine, showed me that with God, anything is possible, even when the odds seem stacked against you.

President Donald J. Trump and Moses Heredia, Coachella, California

These examples, whether from the world of sports, politics, or business, demonstrate the power of persistence, faith, and trust that God can open doors you never imagined. It's the same lesson that Matthew 19:26 teaches.

Obstacles are often man-made, but God has given us the power to overcome them. That's why I tell entrepreneurs to hold fast to their faith. Life and business are filled with setbacks, but persistence is key. People like Stallone, Jordan, and Winfrey didn't let rejection stop them, and neither should you. Every entrepreneur faces challenges, but those who are consistent, proactive, and dedicated to the grind eventually break through.

So, to anyone who feels discouraged or feels like they're up against something they can't beat, I say this: Keep going. Don't give up. The obstacles you face may seem insurmountable, but they are often opportunities in disguise. If you have faith, you will find a way.

And for those who may be skeptical, I encourage you to at least give faith a chance. Even if you don't believe in God right now, I can tell you from personal experience that miracles are real. I've witnessed them in my own life and in the lives of others. Sometimes, it's not just about what you can do—it's about what God can do through you when you trust Him.

So, keep pushing forward, even when it feels like the odds are against you. God's got a way of making the impossible possible, and He can do the same for you.

---

**Axiom:** NOTHING IS IMPOSSIBLE.

**Bible Verse:** *"Jesus looked at them and said, 'With man this is impossible, but with God all things are possible.'"*
— Matthew 19:26 NIV

## GOD IS REAL

As I look back on my journey, I can confidently say that God is real, and He keeps me grounded. I wouldn't be where I am today without His guidance, provision, and miracles. From the small prayers that have been answered to the big moments that shaped my path, I see His hand in everything.

A defining moment in my life was when Sister Palmer prayed over my mom's house, a property I was struggling to secure. It was a miracle that God worked through her prayers. But this wasn't the only time God intervened. Before I even started my own company, Sister Palmer also shared a prophetic word with my sister. She told her that I was going through a transitional phase and that I wouldn't continue in my current position with the company I had been with for over ten years. She said I was meant to go out on my own, to start my own business. At the time, I didn't fully understand it, and I didn't listen. But, just a couple of months later, that's exactly what happened. I left my job, and I started my own company. And I've been in business ever since.

That moment and many others are a reminder that God has been leading me all along. There have been many times when I've prayed for wisdom, health, courage, and direction, and I've seen Him deliver. There is no doubt in my mind—God is real, and nothing is impossible with Him. I've seen miracles unfold in my personal life and my business, and I give Him all the glory for the success I've experienced.

One of the most important things I've done in my life and my business is to continue to honor God. I still pray—both privately and with my team. Every Monday and Friday, we invite anyone in the company who wants to join us in prayer. It's not mandatory, but it's a way for me to give back to God and acknowledge that without Him, I wouldn't have the opportunities and success that I do today.

Entrepreneurs, I want you to remember this: God is the source of all blessings and success. I know it might seem difficult to take time out of your busy schedule for faith and prayer, but trust me—it keeps you grounded. Surrounding yourself with leaders and faith-driven individuals will help you stay focused and aligned with your purpose. I've learned that being a Christian isn't about being perfect—it's about constantly striving to be better, day by day, and keeping your heart aligned with God's will.

Being a Christian means acknowledging God's power and sovereignty over every area of your life—business included. And if you're reading this and you're not sure where you stand with your faith, I encourage you to take a step forward. John 3:16 says, *"For God so loved the world that He gave His one and only Son, that whoever believes in Him shall not perish but have eternal life."* All you need to do is believe in your heart and confess with your mouth that Jesus is Lord. If you're ready, all it takes is a simple prayer: "Jesus, come into my life. I believe in you. I surrender my life to you. Please forgive me of all my sins. I trust you."

Having a relationship with God has completely transformed my life and business. And I truly believe that if you give it all to Him, He will help you navigate the obstacles, make the impossible possible, and bless you beyond what you can imagine.

As I wrap up this section of the book, I want to leave you with this: Nothing is impossible with God. He has been the driving force behind every success and every victory in my life. And I pray that, through this book, you too will see that with faith, dedication, and God's help, there are no limits to what you can achieve.

# PART THREE
# GET A GOAL AND GO ALL IN

# CHAPTER 13
# FOLLOWING MY GUT

*"Now faith is the assurance of things hoped for,
the conviction of things not seen."*
— Hebrews 11:1 ESV

In my early twenties, I was doing well. By twenty-four years old, I was already making six figures and gaining recognition for my hard work. I remember picking up executives from the airport—people in their fifties and sixties—and hearing them say things like, "Moses, you've got a good head on your shoulders for a twenty-four-year-old. I can see it. When you're my age, you'll be someone. You'll be a millionaire." At the time, I knew I had potential, but hearing it from people with years of experience added validation that I was on the right track.

By twenty-eight, I had built a successful team as a regional manager. We had a great recipe for success, and I'd maintained that role for a decade, guiding my team to shine and achieve great things together. It was then that I was offered the vice president position in Louisville, Kentucky. It was a prestigious opportunity, and on paper, it seemed like the next step up.

But before I made any decisions, I turned to my faith. I knew God had always led me in the right direction, so I called Sister Palmer, as I always did when I needed guidance. She told me not to take the promotion and instead urged me to start my own company.

At first, I couldn't see it. I was so ingrained in my current position that I couldn't imagine stepping away from the security and comfort it offered. I felt obligated to stay where I was. It took months of internal struggle before I finally made the decision to explore the alternative.

I knew branching off on my own would be risky, so I consulted with a few trusted people. First, I went to my CPA. He'd known me for nineteen years, doing my tax returns, and I thought he'd understand my potential. But when I presented my plan to him—saying I wanted to withdraw my 401(k) and start my own business—he looked at me and said, "I don't agree with what you are doing. I don't think that's a smart decision. You're doing well at a young age and making great money. I can't advise you to do that."

I left that meeting feeling confused, but I thought, *maybe he's right.* He knows my finances better than anyone. For a second opinion, I went to my accountant. He knows me very well, and in the past, he was a pastor, and I felt very comfortable with him as a father figure. His name was Donald B. Kennedy. Again, the advice was the same: "Don't take the risk and withdraw your 401(k). I can't advise you to go in that direction."

I was frustrated. I thought for sure one of these advisors would tell me to go for it, to bet on myself. So, I went to one more person: an attorney I had met through the car accident who had become a friend. I thought for sure he'd encourage me. But when I showed him my plan, he laughed and said, "Moses, I think I'm in the wrong business because if this really works, you would be making way more money than me. I can't advise you to go this route."

That was the moment I realized I was asking the wrong people for advice. I was looking for validation from others who weren't taking the same risks I was willing to take. What I needed to do was ask God and bet on myself. So, I did what I should have done in the first place: I got on my knees and prayed.

I prayed to God and asked the Holy Spirit for His guidance and wisdom. And that's when I decided to go all in. I turned down the vice president position and made the bold decision to start my own company. I bet on myself—and I committed to the goal I had set: to build something from the ground up that I could call my own.

In life, people will always try to feed you their doubts. They'll tell you it's too risky, that you're not ready, that you should stay comfortable where you are. But I believe Hebrews 11:1 says, *"Now faith is the assurance of things hoped for, the conviction of things not seen,"* as well as Matthew 7:7, which says, *"Knock, and the door will be opened to you; seek, and you will find; ask, and it will be given to you."*

And that's exactly what I did. I knocked, I sought, and I asked. I asked God to open the door, and He did. Looking back now, I can tell you that betting on yourself is one of the best decisions you can make.

Here's the thing—whatever you're after, there's never a "right time" to start. If you're waiting for the right moment, you'll be waiting forever. There's always a reason to hold back, but you can't let that stop you. All you need is a solid plan, a proven concept, and the patience to start slow. You have to be mindful, consistent, and always deliver on your promises.

Just like Blind Bartimaeus in the Bible, when everyone else around him told him to be quiet when he was crying out to Jesus to restore his eyesight, he cried out even louder, "Jesus, Son of David, have mercy on me!" And Jesus healed him.

Bartimaeus didn't let the voices around him dictate his destiny. He took a step of faith, and he was rewarded.

Just like Bartimaeus, you need to take that step of faith. You may not see the full picture, but trust that when you step out, God will be there to guide you. You just have to bet on yourself. There will never be a perfect time, but only by betting on yourself can you make your dreams a reality.

> **Axiom:** BET ON YOURSELF.
>
> **Bible Verse:** *"Now faith is the assurance of things hoped for, the conviction of things not seen."*
> — Hebrews 11:1 ESV

## CHAPTER 14
## GROWING FROM THE GROUND UP

*"So do not lose your bold, courageous faith;*
*for you are destined for a great reward."*
— Hebrews 10:35 TPT

In late October 2003, after ten years with the company that gave me my first job and my first paycheck, I turned down the vice president of sales opportunity, resigned from my position as regional manager, and cashed in my 401(k). I was ready to start Global Processing Systems, but I had no clear path forward. That company had been my only job up until that point, and I didn't have an official business plan, a company checking account, or even an office. But I wasn't going to let that stop me—I had hustle, and that was enough to get started.

For the first three months, I held sales meetings wherever I could—usually in the parking lot of gas stations off the freeway. I met at restaurants, coffee shops, and anywhere in Southern California where I could connect with my sales agents. I wanted to sell them on the dream of making residuals, or ongoing commission that wasn't offered to agents at the time. With me, as long as the customer was processing with us, the agent would get an ongoing commission. I was determined to make it work, no matter what I had to do. In January, I rented an 800-square-foot conference room for one thousand dollars a month. It was far from glamorous—just a small cubicle for me and a reception area for my agents to drop off deals or fax in their paperwork. But it was a step forward, and I believed it would lead to more sales.

At the time, I didn't have a lot of resources, so everything I made went back into the business. There was no salary for me the first three years. It was a grind. I spent fourteen to eighteen hours a day building the company, often working weekends, and everything I earned went right back into advertising, hiring, and growing the company. I was recruiting constantly, thinking outside the box, and hiring anyone I could find. It was all about getting the business off the ground.

Ribbon Cutting Ceremony – Global Processing Systems, San Dimas Location

> Donald B. Kennedy—MBA
> Management Services
>
> *Don met Moses in 2005 when Moses was first starting Global Processing Systems.*
>
>
>
> "I've known Moses since 2005, when I started working at Cheatham Associates. He was one of my first clients. Back then, his business, Global Processing, was still a sole proprietor, and he asked me to help incorporate it, which we did. Over the years, I helped him incorporate several other businesses, including a property management company and a boxing management venture.
>
> Throughout the process, Moses showed a rare combination of humility and intelligence. He's the kind of guy who would rather give credit to others for his success than take any for himself. I remember when he first started his business, he didn't pay himself a salary, because he didn't care about money—he just cared about building the business. Moses always had a plan, a strategy to succeed, and a way to make those around him successful, too. One example of his foresight was when he decided to stop selling equipment and instead focus on long-term service contracts, a move that initially seemed crazy but ultimately turned out to be brilliant. Moses's ability to see opportunities others miss has been key to his success. In fact, I believe he's cornered the market for Latino-owned businesses in Southern California when it comes to card processing services, because he saw a need that commercial banks were ignoring."

As the company grew, so did the need for more space. I remember knocking on the door of the office next door to mine. The tenant had a small space, and I was able to buy them out and expand into that area. It was a modest office at first, but as we continued to recruit and grow, we needed more room. So I did what I had to do—kept expanding. I knocked down walls, merged suites, and slowly built a larger team. By 2008, I had knocked down four suites and grown the business to a point where we had a boardroom, multiple offices, and cubicles for the expanding staff. That's the reality of growth: it's not always linear, and it certainly isn't easy.

But this growth wasn't just about expanding physical space. It was about establishing a culture of trust and commitment—and that was something I built into the foundation of the company. From the start, I believed that the customer is the boss. It was a principle I carried into every meeting, every training session, and every deal. I knew that if we took care of our customers, they'd take care of us. Our clients weren't just numbers; they were the ones who paid our bills, and we had to honor that relationship. This philosophy shaped our company and led to the long-term success we've had.

I remember hosting those early meetings—sometimes in restaurants, sometimes in parks. I'd bring a whiteboard to sketch out the business model and share the vision for the company. Some of my agents didn't understand the formula I was explaining, but they trusted me. And they did. Those agents who took a leap of faith with me in the early days are still with the company today—many of them have flourished. They've bought homes, sent their kids to college, and built families. Some started on commission-only, and now they're key players in the business. That's a testament to the culture we built from the ground up.

When I decided to start my own company, it wasn't just a leap of faith—it was a decision to embrace the long, challenging, and often slow journey that comes with entrepreneurship.

In those early days, everything felt like a hustle. Growth wasn't going to happen overnight. I knew that. But I also knew that the only way to build something lasting was to start and take that first step. I didn't expect instant success; I knew it was going to take time, effort, and a lot of perseverance.

One thing I learned quickly is that everything great takes time. Success isn't a sprint; it's a marathon. Whether you're starting a business or chasing any other big dream, the journey isn't linear, and it certainly isn't instant. It's easy to get caught up in the idea that growth should happen quickly, but if you look at the most successful people—take Colonel Sanders, starting KFC in his sixties—they didn't get there fast. It took them years of hard work and consistency.

Al Arriola—National Sales Director, Global Processing Systems

*Al met Moses in 2008 when he was looking for new cars to wash.*

"I first met Moses about seventeen years ago when I was washing cars and looking for work. I walked into his office, offering to clean their cars for free, and they gave me a shot. I didn't know what they did at the time, just that they had nice cars, and I needed the work. It wasn't until a few years later, when I was desperate for a job, that I reached out to Moses. He remembered me and offered me a position, even though I didn't know much about the business. I started cleaning machines and slowly began to learn about credit card processing. Moses took me under his wing, teaching me everything I needed to know about the industry, from reading statements to understanding fees. When it comes to understanding how to make things work, he's a genius. He shows you how to do things in a way that's not always obvious, like how to get the same result with a different approach, or how to make a customer feel truly valued. But despite all his success, he never flaunts it—he's always willing to teach and guide others. He made me who I am today."

The key to success isn't about finding shortcuts or taking the easy route; it's about putting in the time, staying consistent, and trusting the process. Yes, there were times when I felt like I was spinning my wheels. But I stayed focused on my vision, even when it felt like growth was moving too slowly. Over time, things started to click. As we began to gain momentum, I realized that success wasn't about hitting a big milestone in a short amount of time; it was about building something solid, brick by brick, even when it didn't seem like much was happening. As long as I stayed disciplined, stayed grounded, and stayed focused on the long-term vision, I knew the business would eventually get where it needed to go.

And that's what makes success so rewarding—when you've put in the time, stayed consistent, and pushed through the tough times, you get to look back and see how far you've come. The growth isn't always obvious in the moment, but if you trust the process and remain dedicated to the journey, it will eventually show itself.

In the end, it's not about taking shortcuts. It's about understanding that everything worthwhile requires time and effort. Every success story is a story of perseverance, consistency, and patience. There will be ups and downs, twists and turns—but if you stay focused, the results will come. And when they do, you'll know that all the hard work, all the sacrifices, and all the waiting were worth it.

Because, as I learned along the way—everything great takes time. But with that time, and the dedication to stick with it, success is inevitable.

---

**Axiom:** TAKE RISKS.

**Bible Verse:** *"So do not lose your bold, courageous faith; for you are destined for a great reward."*
— Hebrews 10:35 TPT

## CHAPTER 15
## BETRAYAL IS INEVITABLE

*"Be kind and compassionate to one another, forgiving each other, just as in Christ God forgave you."*
— Ephesians 4:32 NIV

In every line of business and in every industry, you will come across unfaithful and dishonest people. It's an unfortunate truth.

Before I officially started my company, when I was still in the planning stages and right before I resigned from my previous job, I held several meetings with a small group of people I trusted. These were individuals I knew well, and I shared my vision for the business with them. I explained how we would execute the plan and developed a business model that I put a lot of time and thought into. I only shared this with people I felt completely comfortable around.

What I didn't know at the time, though, was that there was a mole in my midst. One of the individuals who attended these meetings seemed loyal, but behind my back, he was gathering information. Unbeknownst to me, this person took everything I had shared: my business model, the steps I planned to take, even the marketing materials, business cards, and the vision for the company. He started gathering everything, including the concept of how I was planning to establish the company, the timeline, and everything else.

I remember one instance clearly: we had a company meeting at Las Brisas in Laguna Beach. At the time, I didn't have an office, so I treated my team to lunch, and we met in the conference room. This individual was there, but he disappeared halfway through the meeting. That's when I started feeling like something wasn't right.

Weeks later, this person opened up his own business using the exact plan I had laid out. It was devastating—not just because he took my ideas, but because I had known him for many years, and he was like family to me. It felt like a betrayal, just as Judas betrayed Jesus, and it hurt—I'm sure there are other business owners who have experienced this.

So, what did I do? I didn't waste my energy on him. Instead of focusing on trying to stop him or get back at him, I redirected my energy into improving my own business plan, tightening it up, and being more cautious with who I shared it with going forward.

A year later, I found out through the grapevine that his business had failed. But that wasn't the point for me. The lesson here is this: no one can steal your dream or your vision. They can take your ideas, your plan, even your words, but they can never live your dream because you're the one who created it. People can mimic the surface, but they can't replicate the passion, the drive, or the grit that you put into it.

In this case, I chose not to entertain the negativity or waste my time trying to bring him down. Instead, I stayed focused on what I was building. I didn't let the betrayal derail me. Yes, it was hurtful, but I knew that God had given me a gift, and I wasn't going to let someone else's actions prevent me from pursuing it. I kept pushing forward and trusted that everything would work out in the end.

And in the end, it did. God handled the situation. I stayed true to the vision and kept moving forward. Everything has a season. That betrayal was temporary, and just like any trial or obstacle in life, it too would pass. The important thing is to take those challenges as learning experiences and use them to keep growing and moving in the right direction.

There are always two paths you can take when faced with adversity. You can let it eat you alive, distract you, and hinder your growth, or you can learn from it and continue forward. I chose to stay focused, remain positive, and stay productive. I kept my eye on my goal. It wasn't just about me—it was about the people who were depending on me, the clients who were trusting us, and the employees who were working hard alongside me. I had a responsibility to stay focused, to lead by example, and to stay disciplined in the pursuit of our goals.

It was easy to get sidetracked by negativity or let this betrayal ruin everything. But I made a conscious decision to rise above it. My goal was clear: I was building something for the future, not just for myself, but for my staff and clients. I could have let this incident pull me off course, but I didn't. Instead, I doubled down on my efforts, stayed disciplined, and remained committed to the vision.

Ephesians 4:32 says, *"Be kind and compassionate to one another, forgiving each other, just as in Christ God forgave you."* Forgiveness is a powerful thing. It's not about forgetting the hurt, but about not letting it consume you. I chose to forgive the person who betrayed me, and I continue to choose forgiveness in all aspects of my life. Just like Jesus forgave, I forgive. It's important to not let bitterness or resentment hold you back, because holding on to those feelings only harms you in the long run.

Take your experience, learn from it, and continue to move

forward with a positive, proactive, and productive attitude. There's always going to be obstacles, but it's how you respond to them that makes all the difference. Stay grounded in your goals, stay disciplined, and keep moving forward. Because if you do, no one can take your dream away from you.

> **Axiom:** FORGIVE AND FORGET.
>
> **Bible Verse:** *"Be kind and compassionate to one another, forgiving each other, just as in Christ God forgave you."*
> — Ephesians 4:32 NIV

# CHAPTER 16
# OVERCOMING OBSTACLES

*"Blessed is the man who remains steadfast under trial for when he has stood the test. He will receive the crown of life, which God has promised to those who love him."*
— James 1:12 NIV

I remember how well we were doing year after year. We were grinding, progressing, and scaling, and profits were steadily rising. Everything seemed to be going in the right direction—until the stock market crash of 2008.

That year, we saw a massive increase in calls, but at the same time, we began receiving a lot of cancellations. Business owners and retailers were struggling to keep their doors open. People were losing their homes. Many of our customers had purchased homes at a certain interest rate, but when the real estate and financial markets crashed, their interest rates ballooned, and they couldn't afford the monthly payments. On top of that, the properties were worth less than the loans they had taken out. People were walking away from their homes, and the banks were repossessing properties, boarding them up. It was chaotic, it was heartbreaking, and it affected our company tremendously.

We weren't growing steadily anymore. Everything came to a halt. We weren't seeing the same profits, and cancellations were coming in faster than ever. Truthfully, things were tight, and I knew we had to pivot if we were going to survive.

As the owner and CEO, I had to think of new strategies to keep the company afloat. We made cuts across the board. We pressed pause on company functions. We stopped buying supplies.

But that wasn't enough. So, we took it a step further. We stopped giving raises and bonuses. We stopped hiring new staff. I even made the decision to stop taking a salary myself, redirecting that money to the staff so that no one had to be let go.

Still, it wasn't enough. That's when I had the idea to shift our offerings to better align with what customers needed in the current market. One of our clients at the time needed a paper supplier for receipts, so we started offering that. It wasn't about being a sales company anymore—it became about customer service. We were just trying to meet whatever needs our clients had because we needed every bit of revenue we could get.

At the same time, I was still doing everything I could to help our customers who were on the verge of canceling. Many of them were losing their homes and businesses, so I lowered fees and helped them maintain their services where I could. Some of them managed to climb out of their financial troubles, but sadly, many others lost not only their homes but also their businesses. That's when I realized the massive need for real estate, especially as people were losing so much.

That's when my brother Rafael and I decided to open M&R Properties.

By this time, I had enough money saved up to invest in real estate. We began buying duplexes, residential homes, and businesses—particularly those in apartment complexes that were in default or about to foreclose. It was a devastating time for many, but for those who had the capital to take advantage of the situation, there were opportunities to be had. I've always believed in making the most of the opportunities that come my way, and I wasn't about to miss out.

Today, that real estate business is still thriving, and I'm incredibly blessed that I was able to pivot during that tough period.

It wasn't until 2012 that I started to see the market shift and make a positive turn for businesses and owners—Global Processing Systems included. By that point, we were able to start recruiting and hiring again. And in 2014, I moved the company from San Dimas to a bigger facility in La Verne—more square footage, more room to grow. From there, our growth accelerated quickly. Not only did we get back to where we were before the crash, but we doubled our previous success. People were no longer afraid to spend or buy. The banks had become more careful, conducting due diligence, improving their underwriting, and asking for more proof of financials. All of this helped stabilize the economy and banking system.

And while the economy was recovering, many of my competitors were eliminated in the wake of the crash. With large corporations failing and banks seizing assets, many of their employees came looking for a place to work. So, we took them in.

We had God to thank for the way we were able to bounce back when so many others couldn't. Not only did we survive, but we thrived. And for seven years, we continued to grow and expand.

In 2020, COVID-19 hit—a blow not just to the United States but to the entire world. Like so many other non-essential businesses, we were forced to close our office. For fourteen months, we had to operate remotely, and during that time, we lost some employees who didn't want to adapt to the new situation.

Once again, I knew we had to do something differently, to pivot once more, and we decided to restructure and adapt by offering point-of-sale systems to restaurants that offered delivery. Of course, everything had to be done remotely via Zoom—something that was completely new to us, just like it was for many other businesses. It wasn't ideal, and it was definitely less personal, but it was the best we could do. We hung on and stayed consistent, doing what we could to keep things moving forward.

It felt like one obstacle after another. But because we were able to find a solution time and time again, we survived. We adapted to the circumstances, stayed resilient, and, by the grace of God, we're still standing today to tell the tale.

What separated me from others during tough times, like the crash and the pandemic, was my faith. I never took my foot off the pedal. James 1:12 reminds us to remain steadfast under trial, knowing that perseverance will eventually lead to success. This mindset, staying faithful and consistent through hardships, is something I've carried with me every day, and it's what helped me weather the storms—whether in business or in life.

In my experience, selfish people don't do well because they're only focused on themselves. I've always made my customers and staff my first priority. I've always been the last one to take a salary, the first one to take the hit when things aren't going well. I've always carried the weight before my staff or clients feel it. It's been my philosophy from day one: be obsessed with making others successful, and everything else will fall into place. Over time, the rewards will come.

But the most important thing, especially when it comes to dealing with challenges, is finding the solution. Everyone, in business and in life, faces roadblocks. The difference is how you handle them. What I always tell my staff is, "If you come to me with a problem, come with a solution first."

I want them to think critically. What's your solution? How can we fix it? Because there's always a way to solve a problem—there's always a solution. Sometimes they don't have an answer, and that's when I step in to coach them through it. But more often than not, I want them to come to me with their ideas first. My job isn't to always give the answer. It's to help them develop their own problem-solving skills, build leadership, and create a mindset of innovation.

I've been hit with many challenges over the years. And let me tell you, you're always going to face problems. It's not the problems themselves that define you—it's how you deal with them. I believe ninety percent of success is in how you handle the challenges that come your way. The other ten percent is finding the right solution. And even if you don't have the perfect answer at first, that's okay. The key is to stay adaptable. You can always pivot and keep moving forward.

As an entrepreneur, if you stop thinking creatively, you'll stop growing. If you stop innovating, you'll go out of business. The world doesn't wait, and your competitors certainly won't. Customers are always looking for the best products and services, and if your competition is offering something faster, better, or more innovative, they'll choose them over you.

So, don't ever stop thinking about how you can improve. Never stop looking for new ways to add value and scale your business month after month, year after year. If you don't put the thought and leadership into your business, you won't be able to keep up with your competitors. Keep moving forward, keep evolving, and continue to find the solution, because that's what will keep you thriving.

> **Axiom:** FIND THE SOLUTION.
>
> **Bible Verse:** *"Blessed is the man who remains steadfast under trial for when he has stood the test. He will receive the crown of life, which God has promised to those who love him."* — James 1:12 NIV

# GET A GOAL AND GO ALL IN

No one told me when I was seventeen years old to leave my mom or the place I was born and raised. I wasn't being challenged, and I was getting into trouble. Ultimately, I knew I had to build a better life for myself. My biggest goal became to leave, because deep down, I knew that if I didn't, I'd never accomplish anything else. So, I did.

My biggest piece of advice to you is this: don't let anything stop you from achieving your goals. Taking risks, whether big or small, is scary, but it's what leads to the biggest rewards. If I hadn't taken those risks, I wouldn't be where I am today. I wouldn't have gotten my first job, been promoted, started my business, or even written this book. Each step, no matter how small, was a risk. But I went after it because I knew my goals were worth the effort.

When I withdrew my 401(k) to start Global Processing Systems, there was no turning back. I had no alternatives. My goal was clear, and I was going to accomplish it. I went all in, betting on myself and creating my own opportunities, even when they seemed nonexistent.

Then came the 2008 market crash. Most people would have

waited for things to work themselves out or for the economy to recover, but I didn't sit idle. I didn't hope things would magically improve. Instead, I pivoted. I changed our offerings. I started new businesses. My focus stayed on my goal, and I exerted one hundred percent to make sure we didn't stray off course. There was no Plan B. There was only Plan A, and I was determined to make it work.

To achieve any goal, you have to give one hundred percent. There's no room for half-effort. You can't show up with only twenty, thirty, or fifty percent and expect success. If you're not willing to go all in—mentally, physically, emotionally, and financially—then you shouldn't do it at all. I've learned that the hard way, but I've also learned that going all in, without fear, is what separates the successful from the ones who give up.

I had a great example of fearlessness in my mother. She did everything in her life without hesitation—starting her own business, moving to a new country, taking chances on people, and betting on herself. I watched her face adversity head-on and never back down. And I realized that if I wanted to be successful, I had to do the same. Fear doesn't help you achieve your goals; taking action does.

So, as you work toward your own goals, don't wait for it to be handed to you. Don't sit around hoping things will magically get better. A goal worth fighting for is a goal worth working toward, and it's one you must actively pursue. If you do that, there's nothing that can stop you from achieving what you've set out to do.

# PART FOUR
# GO GLOBAL

# CHAPTER 17
# FACING GRIEF

*"In all things God works for the good of those who love him, who have been called according to his purpose."*
— Romans 8:28 NIV

Rewinding to February 2004, I had just opened the office for my new company about a month earlier. The pressures of getting everything off the ground were already weighing on me when, one morning, I was driving to meet my CPA. As I was on my way, I received a call from my dad. His voice was strange—mumbled, almost incoherent. I could tell immediately that something was wrong. The only part I could make out was that my mom wasn't there with him. I kept asking, "What do you mean she's not there? She's not with you? Where is she?" Finally, through his sobs, he told me she passed.

At first, I didn't believe it. I yelled at him, "What are you talking about? Stop telling me something that's not true!" In a daze, I turned the car around, made a U-turn, and drove home, desperate to figure out what was really going on.

When I pulled into the driveway, my brother must have sensed something was wrong. As soon as I stopped, he ran out to meet me and asked what had happened. I couldn't even speak. I just threw my phone at him and said, "Mom... Mom." That's all I could say—I was completely numb.

I remember going to the backyard after that. I was overwhelmed with grief and rage, and I started destroying everything I could find—patio furniture, chairs, tree branches. I was screaming at God, asking why He had taken my mom from me. My clothes were torn, my hands were cut, and I was covered in tears. It was raw, uncontrollable emotion.

When I finally calmed down enough to think straight, I booked a flight back to New Mexico for the next morning.

When I landed, I rented a car and drove straight to my sister's house. As I pulled into the driveway, my father and sister came running out to meet me. They both embraced me tightly, sobbing uncontrollably. Even though I was falling apart inside, I knew I had to be strong for them. I slipped into business mode, asking where my mom was. They gave me the address, and my sister and I decided to drive there together.

I remember being at the funeral home, talking to the person in charge of selecting caskets, flowers, and the service details. He was trying to upsell everything—pushing higher-end caskets, more elaborate flowers, and extra services. Without thinking, I found myself negotiating, asking about pricing, discounts, and trying to cut a deal. And then it hit me. I was standing there, negotiating over my mom's casket and funeral arrangements.

I froze for a moment, realizing what I was doing. I walked out of the room and went to the next, where I turned to my sister. I told her to go back in, pick whatever she wanted, and not to worry about the cost. I'd take care of it. She just needed to make sure everything was right for Mom.

Everything about it felt like a dream—or rather, a nightmare. To be honest, I remember very little of that day. I do remember, though, right before we closed the casket, I placed my favorite necklace in it. I wanted my mom to take something of mine with her, something I truly cherished. After that, my brothers and I, along with three of my cousins, helped load my mom into the hearse and drive to the cemetery.

I also remember the drive to the cemetery. It was daylight, right in the middle of the day. I remember cars pulling over, stopping in their tracks, and turning on their headlights in respect. I remember my childhood friends coming to the service, bringing food. These simple acts of kindness meant more to me than I could express at the time.

After I flew back to California, the pain was overwhelming. I buried myself in my work, trying to shut out everything I felt. It was like diving into the ocean and never coming up for air. For years, I pretended my mom was still alive, never truly accepting her passing. Instead, I channeled all my energy into my work. Work became my distraction.

I worked long hours—fourteen, sixteen, sometimes eighteen-hour days, day in and day out. The company was so new at the time, and I needed to stay focused. But more than that, I didn't want to confront the pain of losing my mom. By staying busy, I could avoid thinking about her death. But I knew I couldn't avoid it forever. Eventually, I would have to face it. Ten years passed, and every time I thought of my mom, or was reminded of her, I would feel the emotional weight building up. But no matter how hard I tried, I couldn't suppress the grief any longer. It was time to deal with it.

Roses placed in memory of Elestina Heredia, Moses Heredia's mother, February 19, 2014—ten years after her passing

Rafael Heredia, Cenia Heredia, Moses Heredia, Rigo Heredia, and Moses Heredia Sr.

So, I decided to see a therapist. She helped me peel away the layers of my grief, one by one. Instead of avoiding it, I worked through it. On the tenth anniversary of my mom's death, I held my own ceremony by the ocean. I brought twelve roses with me, and for each one, I threw it into the water at Dana Point, taking a moment to thank my mom for the lessons she had taught me:

*Thank you for teaching me work ethic.*
*Thank you for teaching me how to bless others.*
*Thank you for teaching me to believe in myself.*

*Thank you for teaching me to be unafraid, to be compassionate, to be selfless, to be a successful businessman.*

*Thank you for teaching me to have a big heart, to be considerate of others, and to give back to the community.*

*Thank you for teaching me to be a better man.*

Without my mother, there would be no global impact on my life. If it weren't for her, I wouldn't know what true success feels like. She was not only my greatest teacher but also my best friend.

Romans 8:28 reminds us: *"In all things God works for the good of those who love him, who have been called according to his purpose."* At the time when my mom passed, I couldn't understand why it had to happen. Losing her was devastating, and it felt like the world was coming down around me. But looking back, I can see how God's plan was at work.

When I lost my mom, I had two choices: I could either let the grief crush me, or I could use it as a stepping stone to grow. For a while, I chose to bury myself in work, using it as an escape to avoid the pain. But in the years that followed, God led me to confront that grief. I dealt with it head-on, and it changed me. It made me stronger, more compassionate, and, ultimately, more connected to Him. I believe that God allowed me to experience that loss for a reason, and I wouldn't be the person I am today if it hadn't happened. I believe He was shaping me for something bigger, and His plan was always in motion.

As an entrepreneur or business owner, you will inevitably face challenges. Whether it's the loss of a loved one, a setback in your business, or a personal tragedy, life will hit hard. The key difference between merely surviving and truly thriving is how you respond to those difficulties.

When I lost my mother, the pain never fully went away. But over time, I learned how to live with it. And I came to understand that, just as the Bible teaches us, even our struggles can work for our good.

So, cherish the good times and the people around you. And

when tragedy strikes, don't try to avoid it. It's important to feel the pain. Anger, confusion, and heartbreak are natural responses to loss. But you can't escape grief. It was hard to come to terms with my mother's passing, but when I finally did, I found peace. Process the pain and allow it to strengthen you. Trust in God's plan, even when it doesn't make sense.

Remember, growth often comes through hardship. Every trial you face will shape you into a stronger, more resilient person.

---

**Axiom:** DON'T STOP.

**Bible Verse:** *"In all things God works for the good of those who love him, who have been called according to his purpose."*
— Romans 8:28 NIV

## CHAPTER 18
## GIVE BACK

*"And God is able to bless you abundantly, so that in all things at all times, having all that you need, you will abound in every good work."*
— 2 Corinthians 9:8 NIV

One of the most important lessons I've learned in my life is that true success isn't measured by what you have, but by what you give. To me, success and having a global impact is about the people's lives that God has called us to impact and bless. Growing up, my mother taught me this from an early age. We didn't have much, but we always found ways to help others—whether it was through food, clothes, or simple acts of kindness. She gave, not because she had an abundance, but because she knew what it was like to go without.

When I moved to California at seventeen years old, I couldn't afford much. I remember putting shoes and other essentials on layaway at Miller's Outpost because I simply didn't have the money. Those struggles stayed with me, and they shaped my understanding of wealth.

Brian Hoffman—Owner, The Brass Alligator

*Brian met Moses through a mutual friend and eventually was hired to work for Global Processing Systems.*

"We met back in the early 2000s when I was struggling—working three low-paying jobs and going to community college. I had no direction, but Moses saw something in me. I'll never forget the day he took me shopping at Ross—bought me five shirts, ties, slacks, everything I needed to look professional. He didn't have to do that. But he said to me, 'I want you to see that I just invested in you, and now I want you to invest your time in me.' That moment changed everything for me. He taught me to never stop moving forward, and to always invest in those who invest in you."

So, as soon as I was financially able, I began giving back quietly, like my mother did. I would pay off layaway bills for families who couldn't afford Christmas presents. The families didn't know who was helping them—it was just a way to make a difference. In one instance, I found out later that some of those families were actually my own relatives. It hit me hard. I wasn't just giving to strangers, but to my own flesh and blood. That was a reminder of how interconnected we all are and how we should always look out for each other.

One holiday season, when Walmart stopped doing layaways, I didn't let that stop me from finding a way to help. I contacted my old elementary school and offered to buy $150 gift cards for every child. The principal was shocked by the offer, and after the school approved it, I made the purchase. The impact was immediate: families used the cards for food or small gifts. Some of them even shared their gratitude with the school, which spread the word about the donation.

I've always believed that we shouldn't expect recognition for doing good. My mom taught me that you give because it's the right thing to do, not to get credit. I still choose to give anonymously as much as possible because that's how it feels most authentic to me. But even when you don't seek attention for your generosity, it can have a ripple effect—especially in your community.

Humility is key, and it's something I learned from my mom. No matter how successful she became, she never flaunted it. And I've carried that lesson with me throughout my journey. Success doesn't change who you are; it just amplifies the traits you already have. If you're humble, success will make you more generous. If you're arrogant, it will only make you more so.

That's why I don't talk about my success much. When my old high school friends came to visit me, they were surprised by how far I'd come. They didn't know about my accomplishments because I don't broadcast them. For me, success isn't about showing off; it's about making a positive impact, especially in the lives of others.

Money, on its own, doesn't change you. It just makes it easier to live a more comfortable life—provide better healthcare, put food on the table, and help the people who need it. But wealth isn't the ultimate goal. Health and humility are far more important. I've learned that the hard way. True wealth is having God, health, a strong family, and a spirit of generosity.

In 2 Corinthians 1:3-4, the Apostle Paul says to the church at Corinth that God comforts us in our troubles so that we can comfort others in theirs. This is how I view generosity—it's not just about giving out of surplus, but about understanding the struggles others face and offering what you can to ease their burden. My mother gave, even when she had little to offer. And that's something I try to replicate every day.

When I started my business and gained financial stability, I made it a point to help others who were in need. Whether it was donating to local orphanages, supporting youth programs, or contributing to families who needed a hand during the holidays, I saw it as a responsibility—not just a choice. Giving back has become a core part of my life because I understand what it's like to struggle.

But giving isn't just about money. It's about time, effort, and attention. It's about being present for others when they need you most. Whether it's volunteering at a homeless shelter or supporting a local cause, every little bit helps. You don't have to be wealthy to make a difference; you just have to care.

If you've reached a point in your life or business where you're financially comfortable, I encourage you to use that opportunity to give back. Generosity isn't just a personal choice; it should be part of the DNA of every business. Whether it's donating to a cause you care about or helping out a neighbor in need, don't forget where you came from.

The world often tells us to accumulate wealth and keep it for ourselves, but in Acts 20:35, the Bible also says, "It is more blessed to give than to receive." In believing that, I've been able to impact many lives, both personally and professionally, and for that, I am overflowing with blessings.

If you're fortunate enough to be in a position where you can help, don't hesitate. When you live with generosity in your heart, not only do you enrich others, but you enrich your own life as well. And in the end, that's the kind of success that matters most.

> **Axiom:** BE GENEROUS.
>
> **Bible Verse:** *"And God is able to bless you abundantly, so that in all things at all times, having all that you need, you will abound in every good work."* — 2 Corinthians 9:8 NIV

## CHAPTER 19
## A VISION FOR THE FUTURE

*"Where there is no vision, the people perish."*
— Proverbs 29:18 NIV

In 2023, Global Processing Systems celebrated its twentieth anniversary, and as I reflect on the road we've traveled, I can't help but feel a deep sense of gratitude. Looking back on the lives touched through this business—whether directly through our services or through the impact of our revenue—it's clear that we've been blessed in ways beyond what we could have imagined when we first started. Now, as we look ahead to the next twenty years, I'm excited about the future and the new opportunities we have to make an even bigger impact in the world.

One of our main goals moving forward is to expand Global Processing Systems into new markets across the country. To achieve that, we need the right people—disciplined, dedicated individuals with a desire to succeed. We want to see more people take advantage of the commission opportunities with recurring residual income that our current agents get. We don't cap our agent's commissions; we want to help them achieve wealth and live the American Dream. Our mission is to continue to break records, and I truly believe that the more we grow, the more lives we can change. But beyond just business growth, I also want to help other entrepreneurs create their own global impact. That's why I'm focusing on speaking engagements and podcasting, so I can share the lessons I've learned and help others grow both in business and in faith. It's not just about success in business—it's about aligning our work with our values and using our platforms to inspire others.

Moses Heredia – Keynote Speaker, Sacramento

In addition to speaking and coaching, I'm also preparing to launch a mastermind program where entrepreneurs can come together for monthly coaching sessions and meet both virtually and in person. These gatherings will go beyond just business advice; they'll offer a space for personal development, helping entrepreneurs navigate both their professional lives and the challenges they face on a day-to-day basis. It's about creating a community where we can all learn and grow together.

Marc Dupras - Founder, Dupras Group LLC

*Marc met Moses in 2017 after Global Processing Systems had already taken off.*

"I met Moses in 2017 at the gym we both worked out at in Orange County, and we immediately bonded over our shared discipline and work ethic. He would show up at 5 a.m. every day, and I respected that commitment. We got close quickly, and over the next several months, as I watched him operate and listened to his stories, I became inspired to follow in his footsteps and start my own company. Now, six years in, Moses has been incredibly supportive, always offering genuine mentorship and helping me connect with the right people. Last time Moses was in town, he took my girlfriend and me out to dinner with some of his close friends and family, and that night, it was Moses's hospitality that blew her away. He was the guy serving everyone wine, making sure they were taken care of, and putting others first—literally the kind of guy who eats last. When we left, she told me that nobody—at any dinner event—had ever treated her better. That's just who he is. He wasn't doing it for show; it's in his nature to make others feel valued."

I also have a strong desire to get more involved in politics. In 2024, I became an active delegate for the California State Assembly District Republican Party. Through my experience, I've realized how important it is for business owners to be engaged in the political process. Tax laws, local policies, and regulations affect us in ways we often don't realize, and it's essential to understand how these changes can impact our businesses.

As an entrepreneur, you must stay informed, not just about your industry, but about the laws and people shaping the environment in which you work. It's something I wish I had focused on earlier, and I encourage every entrepreneur to do the same—to understand the systems that govern us and get involved in local politics. It matters more than you might think.

Moses and Rafael Heredia – 2023

Another vision of mine is to continue growing M&R Properties, the company my brother Rafael and I started during the housing crash. Over the years, we've been fortunate to invest in both commercial and residential properties, including building homes from scratch and managing apartment complexes, but we're always looking for new opportunities.

Despite all that's been achieved, the work is never finished. There's always more to be done, more people to help, and more opportunities to grow and give back. That's what excites me. Whether it's expanding my business or continuing my philanthropic efforts, there's always a next step. And for those of you reading this, I encourage you not to limit yourselves. Take advantage of the opportunities that come your way. Success isn't just about making money; it's about creating value, building relationships, and contributing to your community. The road ahead is full of possibilities, and with faith, dedication, and a commitment to giving back, I'm confident that the best is yet to come. Keep striving, keep growing, and keep making a difference. The world needs what you have to offer, and there's no limit to the impact you can make.

I have a picture of my mom in my office and on my phone, reminding me every day that life is not about me. It's about others. It's about giving back. So, I want to encourage you: YES, YOU CAN.

You can do it without education.

You can do it without money.

You can do it no matter the color of your skin.

But...

You cannot do it without God.

You cannot do it without setting a goal.

Elestina Heredia

You cannot do it without the grind.

But with God, Goals, and the Grind, YOU CAN.

If you give it all to God, if you find a gift in the grind, and if you go "all in" with your goals, you will make a global impact.

> **Axiom:** BE OBSESSED WITH SUCCESS.
>
> **Bible Verse:** *"Where there is no vision, the people perish."*
>
> — Proverbs 29:18 NIV

# MOSES'S PROVERBS TO LIVE BY

As you move forward, I want to leave you with some guiding "proverbs" that have shaped my journey—principles I've shared throughout this book, but that I want you to keep in mind as you forge your own path. These ideas have been tested through both successes and setbacks, and they're the foundation on which I've built my life and business.

**1. BE DRIVEN, BE MOTIVATED, AND BE DETERMINED.**

Despite challenges, religion, race, ethnicity, birthplace, education, wealth, or poverty, you are not a victim of circumstance. Anyone, including you, can choose to be driven, motivated, and determined. Make the choice!

**2. BELIEVE IN YOURSELF.**

The only person who can hold you back is you. You are in control of your future. Know and love who you are. Confidence comes from understanding and accepting yourself. When you love who you are, you'll unlock new levels of motivation and strength.

**3. BE COMPASSIONATE.**

Always remain compassionate toward others. No matter how successful you become, never look down on others. Everyone is fighting their own battle, and you never know their struggles. Never judge. Showing compassion to others will always inspire.

**4. BE CONSISTENT.**

Stay consistent in what your focus is, and do not veer off course. Remain consistent and create ways to stay engaged. Show up every day, work steadily and consistently, and it will pay off.

**5. WORK HARD.**

Let this be who you are, not something you did. Whatever you are doing, go all in. Identify your purpose, work hard, commit yourself fully to learn it, and master it.

**6. BE DISCIPLINED.**

This is not just about completing tasks; it is about showing up—staying the course day after day. Discipline builds character. Achieving anything requires discipline. Discipline is what separates dreams from reality.

**7. STAY AWAY FROM SMALL-MINDED PEOPLE.**

Dream big, even if it makes others uncomfortable. Dream so big that it challenges small-minded people. When your vision is bigger than theirs, they won't understand—it's okay. Press forward and encircle yourself with like-minded people. Seek advice from those who have walked the path you want to follow.

**8. STAY FOCUSED.**

Make the choice to step out, pursue something better, and stay focused on it! Block out distractions and stay focused on your goal.

## 9. RECOGNIZE YOUR OPPORTUNITIES.

When recognizing an opportunity, take it. Don't wait for other people's opinions on what they might see. Use your own eyes to see the potential and opportunity in things that arise and seize them.

## 10. DON'T FEEL SORRY FOR YOURSELF.

Don't feel sorry for yourself, no matter how many times you fall or feel like you're failing. Don't get stuck in a bad moment. Realign. A bad day doesn't mean a bad life. Stay positive! Success doesn't come without its challenges. Stay persistent. Persistence is the key. The reward will be worth it!

## 11. MASTER YOUR PASSION.

Discover what your passion is and commit to it one hundred percent. Dedicate yourself one hundred percent to master it.

## 12. NOTHING IS IMPOSSIBLE.

We all have setbacks in our journey. Do not let setbacks, no matter how impactful they seem to be at the time, derail you. Stay committed to your goal. Never lose sight that *all things are possible!*

## 13. BET ON YOURSELF.

Stay true to yourself. Believe in your vision even when others don't. Don't doubt yourself or your abilities. *Always bet on yourself.*

## 14. TAKE RISKS.

Any risk you're avoiding or fearful of could be the one that changes everything! A true leader takes risks. Leaders see the bigger picture and act boldly, even when others doubt them. Don't wait for conditions to be ideal. Take the leap or live with the regret of never having tried.

**15. FORGIVE AND FORGET.**

Holding on to grudges only holds you back. You must let go, forgive, and stay focused on *your* journey, and not on someone else who has wronged you. Forgiveness sets you free to continue forward.

**16. FIND THE SOLUTION.**

Remain steadfast. Think critically. There is always a solution! Allow yourself to be open-minded to seeking other avenues relating to your goal—how to expand or reroute yourself—that will lead to a solution. Everyone faces roadblocks. The key is how you handle them.

**17. DON'T STOP.**

Never stop pushing. It's about refusing to give up. Winners keep going, no matter how hard it gets.

**18. BE GENEROUS.**

Success is measured by many things, not just by what you have but also by what you give. Be generous by using what resources you have to support others with your time, money, effort, and attention. Generosity of any kind will always enrich your own life as well as others'.

**19. BE OBSESSED WITH SUCCESS.**

When you see your potential, the grind becomes addictive. Once you realize how much you're capable of, you won't be able to stop. The grind will fuel you because you know where it can take you. Success to me is like a drug; once you experience it, you'll want more.

# PERSPECTIVE FROM FRIENDS

Anthony Araguz, "Twat," Rob Ridought, "Pickles," and Moses Heredia

**Anthony Araguz, "Twat"**

Moses is one of my best friends—I consider him a brother. We met in high school when he moved to California, and he always looked out for everybody. He had this little ragtop car, and he used to make sure everybody had a ride home.

## PERSPECTIVE FROM FRIENDS

We worked for a detail shop that his brother owned at one time. He didn't know how to detail, but he knew how to work with people. A customer would come in with a problem, and within thirty seconds, he had it figured out. He knew how to talk to people, make them feel good, and earn their trust.

By the end of our senior year, we went to the unemployment office. Moses got a job in telemarketing, and he worked his way up the ladder very quickly.

I'm so proud of the guy. He's the same guy I met in high school, with the same dedication, the same ambition, and the same people skills.

Truthfully, he's changed my life. He doesn't even know how much he continues to impact my daily life, and I'm sure others feel the same way.

Shawn Hills, Moses Heredia, Mike Salas, "Scralge," Anthony Araguz, "Twat," Robert Bustos "Bustos"

**Shawn Hills**

My mom's passing brought Moses and me closer because he had perspective. He lost his mom, too, and since he keeps everything close to the vest, it wasn't until my mom passed that I learned that he went through the same thing.

He was the one person who I could relate to. When you strip everything down, Moses is like a brother to me. Even my wife gets it. Once, she was talking to my fourteen-year-old son, who's having a rough go these days, and she said to him, "Your dad is lucky. Not everybody has the same group of friends they've had for thirty years." I could go anywhere—do anything—and I know I'd have his support. He's kind, funny, smart, and more generous than anyone I've come across. He's so successful, but by no means greedy.

**Rob Ridought, "Pickles"**

I remember in high school, while the rest of us were out partying on the weekend, Moses was working. Then, after high school, we were roommates. He wouldn't usually get home from work until nine o'clock at night, after which he'd go to bed to wake up and do it again. He would do whatever it took to hustle, truly the hardest-working guy I know.

He's also a prankster. He likes to play jokes. One time, we were hanging out and having some beers at my parents' house. I left the room for a minute, and when I came back, my beer tasted like pickles, though since we'd just had hamburgers, I didn't think anything of it. Well, about a week later, I caught them laughing, and they told me they'd put pickle juice in my beer that night. So, they started calling me Pickles.

**Robert Bustos**

I met Moses in the second semester of my junior year. He's always been the guy who would give you his shirt off his back, even if it's all he had. He's just a genuine person.

He did whatever it took to be successful. He broke all types of barriers. And I have to credit a little bit of my career to him because he always told us that if we set our minds to something,

## PERSPECTIVE FROM FRIENDS

we could do it. He said, "You can do it. You just have to put in the work."

### Mike Salas, "Scralge"

I've known Moses since he was broke and didn't have two pennies to rub together. And though he's big on social media, to me, he's still the same guy with the 1970 Honda Civic.

I remember going to his house after his career in sales took off, and I saw he was on the cover of this company leaflet. On the cover it says, *"How do you spell success?"* and it had a picture of Moses with his name spelled M-O-S-E-S. He was killing it right off the bat, and it wasn't too long after that that he decided to branch off and start his own company.

Hector Meneses, "Nector," Anthony Araguz, "Twat," and Moses Heredia

### Hector Meneses, "Nector"

I met him in 1992, in my senior year of high school. He stuck out a little bit, but he was a nice, cool guy. And he was really driven. He had to be.

## PERSPECTIVE FROM FRIENDS

At one point, he worked a commission-only sales job, and he couldn't afford the trash, so he would pile it up. My parents provided me with my first truck, and I remember going to his house to help him get rid of it. He never asked for help, never looked for handouts, but I noticed what he needed and helped him in whatever way I could.

# THANK YOU FOR READING MY BOOK!

### DOWNLOAD YOUR FREE GIFTS
Just to say thanks for buying and reading my book, I would like to give you a free gift, no strings attached!

### Scan the QR Code:

*I appreciate your interest in my book and value your feedback as it helps me improve future versions of this book. I would appreciate it if you could leave your invaluable review on Amazon.com with your feedback. Thank you!*

www.ingramcontent.com/pod-product-compliance
Lightning Source LLC
Chambersburg PA
CBHW020242010526
44107CB00038B/1450/J